Sunrise Montessori
P.O. Box 4077
Napa, Ca 94558
253-1105

Nature
Activities
for
Early Childhood

Janet Nickelsburg

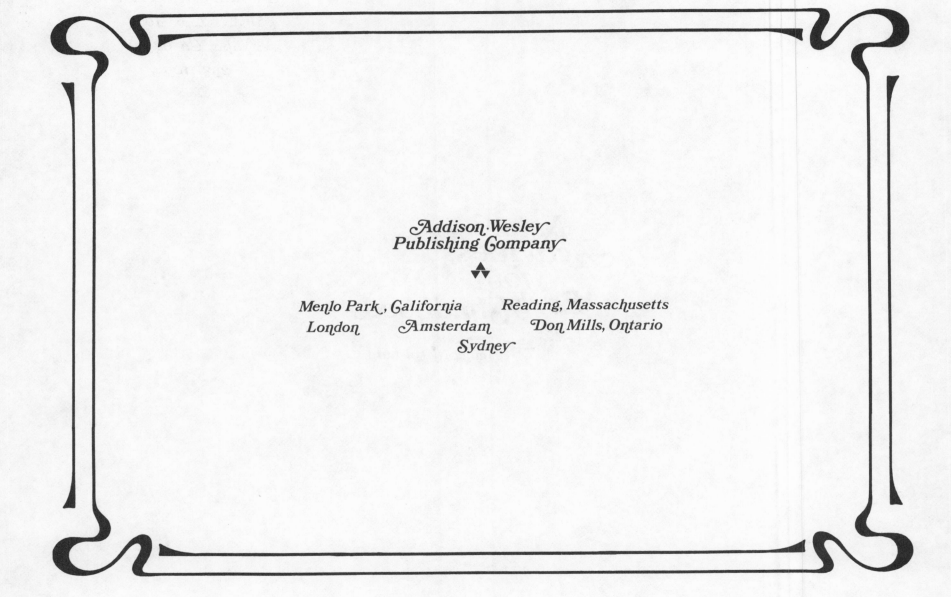

Addison·Wesley
Publishing Company

Menlo Park, California   Reading, Massachusetts
London   Amsterdam   Don Mills, Ontario
Sydney

Nature Activities for Early Childhood

Janet Nickelsburg

To my great grandchildren

This book is in the Addison-Wesley INNOVATIVE SERIES.

ISBN-0-201-05097-8   DEFGHIJK—EB—810798

About The Author

At 83, Janet Nickelsburg is actively involved with nature study organizations, and, as a member of the San Francisco Volunteer Auxiliary, is completing her forty-eighth year of teaching science to young children. In addition to her community activities, Mrs. Nickelsburg writes books, mostly for children and teachers, with the main focus on the environmental sciences. Books she has written include *The Nature Program at Camp, Stargazing and Field Trips* (Burgess Publishing Company), *Ecology, Niches, Habitats, and Food Chains* (J. B. Lippincott Company), and a series of four books called *California from the Mountains to the Sea* (Coward, Mc Cann & Geoghegan, Inc.).

The 250 radio scripts entitled *"Signposts for Young Scientists"* are also the product of Mrs. Nickelsburg's pen. These were broadcast over NBC and received a national award as the best of their kind by the School Broadcast Conference in Chicago. Ten recordings of material rewritten from this show have recently been made available by Educational Activities, Inc., of Baldwin, New York. Mrs. Nickelsburg also conducted a television show for children called *"Stop, Look, and Listen,"* which ran for four years in San Francisco, and she planned and acted as master of ceremonies for an ad-lib radio program in Berkeley called *"The Children's Forum."*

Mrs. Nickelsburg is well known for the service called *"Earth, Sea, and Sky,"* which she conducted over the years for childrens' camps. The program consisted of camp visitation and training of counselors and children for the purpose of setting up a nature program for each camp.

The ease and comfort with which Mrs. Nickelsburg interacts with even the smallest children on field trips, picnics, and other learning situations is an inspiration to all who watch her. Now a great grandmother of nine, it can truly be said that love of children and love of nature have been the two great forces of her life.

Come Out With Me

There's sun on the river and sun on the hill . . .
You can hear the sea if you stand quite still!
There's eight new puppies at Roundabout Farm—
And I saw an old sailor with only one arm!

But every one says, "Run along!"
(Run along, run along!)
All of them say "Run along! I'm busy as can be."
Every one says, "Run along,
There's a little darling!"
If I'm a little darling, why don't they run with me?

There's wind on the river and wind on the hill . . .
There's a dark dead water-wheel under the mill!
I saw a fly which had just been drowned—
And I know where a rabbit goes into the ground!

But every one says, "Run along!"
(Run along, run along!)
All of them say "Yes, dear," and never notice me.
Every one says, "Run along,
There's a little darling!"
If I'm a little darling, why won't they come and see?

From *Now We Are Six* by A. A. Milne, illustrated by
Ernest H. Shepard. Copyright 1927 by E. P. Dutton & Co.,
renewal © 1955 by A. A. Milne. Reprinted by permission
of the publishers, E. P. Dutton & Co., Inc.

Contents

Introduction

ABOUT THE BOOK

This book is designed to help teachers and parents provide young children with experiences in observing nature so as to stimulate children to adventure into the unknown. It is planned to assist children to develop their senses, to sharpen their powers of observation, to improve their speech, and to expand their aesthetic appreciation.

Each of the 44 projects in NATURE ACTIVITIES FOR EARLY CHILDHOOD is a unit in itself. But since each project contains underlying concepts, it can be related to a number of other projects. For example, in observing one animal the children discover something about vision, nutrition, the care and welfare of certain species, and in some cases how other animals have the same characteristics and needs. In plant projects they discover that all plants have certain requirements in common, such as their need for water, sunshine, and freedom from excessive encroachment by animals and other plants. Such concepts as these are freshly defined with each pertinent new project presented.

The most important part of each project is the ACTIVITIES section, by which the children can experience nature directly. The activities suggested are such that you as a teacher or parent will be able to choose those that best fit your children's stage of development. An activity should be presented only when all the materials needed are at hand, and if you feel your children are capable of handling them. Activities better suited for older children are so indicated.

The scientific information at the beginning of each project is meant for the adult and is included to give a little background on the material being discussed. Lists of helpful MATERIALS are provided, along with key VOCABULARY words for the children.

The BIBLIOGRAPHIES at the end of each chapter list books that describe things in simple terms, so that very few scientific books have been included, even in the sections called FOR ADULTS. You will notice that in these sections some of the books are actually childrens' books. These were included because their material is quickly available and clearly stated.

FINDING THE MATERIALS

Many of the living and nonliving things suggested for study in NATURE ACTIVITIES FOR EARLY CHILDHOOD may be found in a nearby field or vacant lot, or even on the school grounds or a backyard. Roaming over a lawn for a half hour, or better still, creeping on hands and knees will turn up many of the things discussed in this book and will provide rewarding experiences in the out-of-doors.

The projects selected deal with animals, plants, or nonliving things common to almost all areas. An earthworm may be found on the sidewalk after a rainstorm or at other times near the surface of the soil; aphids may be studied on a plant growing outside the window; and rain and wind are everywhere!

None of the animals or plants discussed in the book are dangerous to handle. A project on snakes has been omitted, not because all snakes are dangerous, but because of possible confusion between harmless and poisonous snakes. Also, handling a snake is so objectionable to some adults that they may convey their aversion to the children, who may then become prejudiced against snakes. In any event, it is very important not to force children to handle anything they are afraid of. You can sometimes encourage them, however, by inviting them first to touch and later to hold such an animal.

SELECTION OF PROJECTS

Don't feel under any obligation to use more of these projects than are appropriate or available, or to use them in any particular sequence. Projects should be presented one at a time, though several may be running concurrently. There might be a pet, such as a rabbit or a canary, and the children may at the same time be raising plants from seeds or examining the possibilities of a lawn, but each of these projects will have been introduced over a span of time.

WORKING WITH CHILDREN

Because the nature program's principal goal is to encourage children to make their own discoveries, do a minimum of explaining, and then only if asked for. Who knows but that children learn more from silent observations then when a well-meaning adult breaks in and distracts them? Bear in mind that your role in presenting projects should always be that of partner rather than of teacher, for the projects are merely meant to stimulate the child to stop, look, and listen rather than to accomplish specific learning objectives. This is the reason why a heading *Learning Objectives* is not included for each project, for this would place an obligation on you to teach, and might interfere with the children's spontaneous reactions.

It is important for children to experiment in their own ways: what they learn from so doing may be more valuable to them than any project outlined in the book. However, you will do well to stay with the children during each new experience, so as to be on hand to assist them in making their own discoveries. This will enable you to prevent the mishandling of living things.

Because small animals confined in cages require care, the children can help with the filling of food and water dishes, the cleaning of cages, or the holding of animals while their containers are being cleaned. As for the plants, the children will enjoy watering them, picking off dead leaves and flowers, and loosening the soil if it becomes tamped down.

The nature program also offers an opportunity for children to develop their ability to express themselves. The enlarging of vocabulary is an important objective in teaching young children. Offering them objects they can touch and experiment with will give them an incentive for using words new to them so they can share their experiences with others. A Spanish-speaking child in the Head Start Program, after a number of weeks without speaking at all, exclaimed "ojos" while pointing to the eyes of a salamander. "Yes, these are its eyes!", said the teacher. Speech comes naturally in response to a need.

Some children will enjoy making collections of feathers, rocks, pebbles, or seeds, and pressing flowers and leaves and making leaf prints. A nature center to display the childrens' efforts might be set up as an exhibit for other children and visitors.

Nature experiences presented to young children are not intended to be stepping stones to scientific concepts. They are meant to be enjoyed for their own sake. What children learn and later apply to their science courses has only a remote connection with what they are experiencing at the moment. To insist on anticipating the disciplines of tomorrow may spoil the joy of today's experience.

1 Outdoor Group Projects

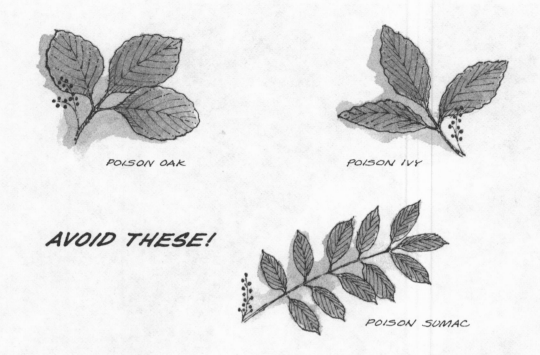

POISON OAK

POISON IVY

AVOID THESE!

POISON SUMAC

Many impressions and learnings come from touching things, as the parent of any young child will attest. Feel walks, like feel books, are not only instructive for young children but fun as well, and should be planned to introduce outdoor experiences to the child.

You might start a feel walk by having the children touch as many different kinds of leaves as they can find. There are leaf edges to run the finger around; there are leaf petioles, or stems, that vary from round to oval to flat. The surfaces of leaves vary in endless ways. They may be sticky, smooth, hairy, furry, prickly, or slimy. The tips of leaves will yield some surprising discoveries to the feeling finger.

Leaves are not by any means the only things in nature that lend themselves to feeling. There are smooth and sharp rocks and pebbles; there is gritty, sandy, and sticky or clayey soil. There are lumpy clods of earth and mud of many sorts—sticky, slimey, watery, etc. Grass too has texture that differs when it is wet and when it is sere.

Manmade objects also have their own textures. Boards do not feel like plaster, concrete differs from both. A metal pipe

SOME HELPFUL MATERIALS

oatmeal boxes, cylindrical objects, assorted socks, man's

KEY VOCABULARY FOR CHILDREN

hairy
hard
prickly
slimy
smooth
soft
sticky

gives a different sensation to the touch than tile or slate. Metal and wooden telegraph poles differ from one another.

There are differences in temperature as well as in texture. A metal pole in the shade feels different from one standing in the sun.

My rubber ball and your tennis ball feel different, your dress and mine, your sweater and mine, your skin and your hair, your lips and your cheeks.

Discovering these sensations can be reinforced by placing a feel box in the school room. Staple a man's sock to the top of a cylindrical box, to conceal the con-tents. Invite the children to feel what is inside. One day there may be a cone, another day a rock and a third, a snail shell. What goes into the feel box should prefera-bly be something the children have already explored on a feel walk.

The feel walk might also be played with objects brought indoors. For this game the children are blindfolded and sit around a table, handing the objects to their neighbor and guessing what they are.

Try the feel game! The children will like it and will learn to enjoy their sense of touch while picking up new words.

3

A Rainy
Day

There are possibilities for nature study even on a rainy day. Falling rain is one portion of the water cycle, which has its origin in the oceans. By evaporation due to the heat of the sun, water vapor rises into the atmosphere, where it cools sufficiently to condense into clouds. From the clouds it falls either directly into the ocean or to earth, and from there a great part of it eventually flows back into the sea. Some of the water evaporates off the land or off standing bodies of water such as lakes and ponds and some from streams. Thus the cycle starts all over again.

ACTIVITIES

1. The cycle of evaporation and condensation can be demonstrated by boiling water in an uncovered pot. The water evaporates because of the heat of the fire and can be condensed into water once more on the bottom of a cold plate held over the pot of boiling water.

2. Look out the window at the clouds on a rainy day and notice that the sky is concealed by a flat layer of clouds (known as stratus clouds). If you look again on a clear day you may see the high, wispy, hairlike clouds (called cirrus), or at other times puffy cumulus clouds.

3. Observe the raindrops on the window pane, their shape, and which portion is brightest. Also look for the dividing line between the light bottom and the dark top. A raindrop is a little lens that reflects objects upside down, so that trees seen through a raindrop appear upside down with their tops near the ground.

4. Watch the raindrop rivulets run down the pane, some moving faster than others, some joining together to form larger streams, and by their added weight breaking away and dashing to the bottom.

5. If the window is screened the drops that reach the glass will be smaller than those that hit the pane directly. Compare this on a screened and unscreened window.

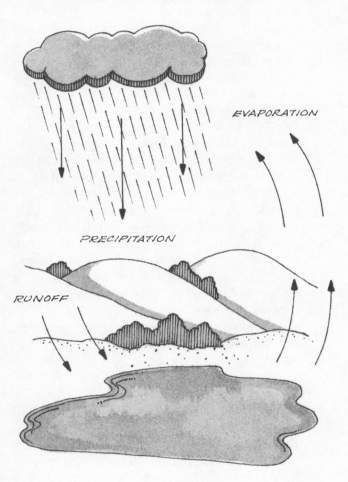

EVAPORATION

PRECIPITATION

RUNOFF

6. Observe the raindrops outside as they hit the ground and notice where they make the biggest splash—on the pavement, on the grass, or on bare soil. Watch the rings formed by raindrops on a puddle or pool.

7. Carry this observation indoors and shake a wet brush over a piece of paper or the bare floor, over a box of soil, and over a box planted with grass.

8. Lay a piece of glass or other smooth-surfaced object in a slanting position and smear oil on one vertical half, leaving the other clean. Notice what effect the oil has on drops of water as they run down. Do the same activity with other liquids, such as vinegar, milk, or molasses. SAFETY NOTE: *Make sure any sharp edges on the piece of glass are covered with tape.*

9. The children should be allowed to dabble their hands in a shallow pan of water and then to shake them over leaves, house plants, paper, and various other substances. They can observe that drops vary in size. It is inevitable that they will scatter some drops on one another too. If allowed to continue only for a few moments the children will get an idea of the way drops feel on the skin.

10. The children can draw cloud pictures, rain falling, and raindrops.

11. A raindrop dance might capture the children's fancy.

12. A later trip to a brookside to continue some of the splashing experiments might be a good follow-up experience.

13. Evaporation can be demonstrated by placing a wet cloth over the warm pavement on a sunny day. Give clothes drying on the line as an example of evaporation.

SOME HELPFUL MATERIALS

boxes
dishes, cold
glass pane, taped edges
hot plate
molasses or syrup
oil
paint brushes
pot of water
soil
vinegar

KEY VOCABULARY FOR CHILDREN

 clouds
*condense
*evaporate
*lens
 raindrops
*water cycle

*Suggested for older children only

The Wind

Wind is simply air in motion, moving from a place of high pressure to one of lower pressure. In other words, since air is a mixture of gases, it can be compressed, and when compressed it is said to have high pressure. Areas of high pressure resist the movement of air into them, and tend to force air outward to areas of lower pressure. As the air flows out of a high pressure area the pressure falls and new air can then move in. Both the outflowing and the influx of air are wind. A body in motion can also produce wind. This is evident to a person in a moving vehicle and to a child running downhill. The air we exhale when we breathe is also wind, and so is air created by an electric or hand fan.

ACTIVITIES

1. The children might observe the movement of smoke as it issues from a chimney (toward the front of a house or to the left of a hill). These directions would be helpful in introducing the concepts of north, south, east, and west.

2. Watch the drift of clouds and the direction in which they are moving. If the wind blowing below, where you are standing, is coming from another direction, the clouds are said to be moved by winds aloft.

3. Go outdoors and notice the direction from which the wind is coming. This will help the children understand that a north wind comes from the north. A wind is named for the direction it comes from, not for where it is going.

4. After observing the direction of the wind, get behind a sheltering wall or fence and notice how the wind is stopped by an obstacle. If the shelter is not at right angles to the direction of the wind, the wind may be deflected or pushed to one side and assume another direction.

5. While running the children will notice the wind on their faces. Then let them draw a cloth or streamer behind them and notice that it is lifted off the ground by the passage of wind below it. This will give them an idea of how an airplane is assisted in remaining aloft.

6. Kite flying may be difficult for little children, but they can try it to show how the wind holds the kite up in the air.

7. Make pinwheels and have the children run with them or blow on them to demonstrate how the wind enters the cupped vanes and spins them around.

8. Blow on a cup of steaming liquid and notice how the steam is blown away by the wind we generate when we blow.

9. Have the children blow on inflated balloons. If a number of children play at blowing them to one another, it will show that the wind can come from different directions.

10. Have the children blow a feather around. This might result in a contest in which each child has his own feather and competes to see which can maintain it in the air longest.

11. Take the feathers outdoors and watch what the wind does to them.

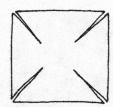

USING SQUARE PIECE*
OF PAPER, CUT SLITS
IN CORNERS A LITTLE
MORE THAN HALFWAY

*ABOUT 25 cm
(10 INCHES) SQUARE

SOME HELPFUL MATERIALS

balloons
cloth streamers
feathers, small
kites (optional)
paper, construction
pins
sticks
water, steaming hot

FOLD ONE CORNER
TO MIDDLE

KEY VOCABULARY FOR CHILDREN

air
east
north
pinwheel
south
west

FOLD ALL ALTERNATE
CORNERS TO MIDDLE

ATTACH TO PENCIL
ERASER WITH TACK,
USING A BUTTON IN
BACK OF PINWHEEL
FOR EASIER
MOVEMENT

Looking
for Spiders

The many kinds of spiders can be differentiated not only by their shape, size, coloration, and habits but also by the kind of webs they build. The garden spiders with striped legs build round, or orb, webs. House spiders build cobwebs, which are more or less sheetlike; grass spiders build a funnel in the ground; dome spiders build a rounded dome under which they lurk; and our only common poisonous spider, the black widow, builds a formless web composed of little pieces running any which way.

The silk the webs are made of issues from little spigot-shaped organs, called spinnerets, situated at the rear end of the spider. As the liquid silk is expelled it hardens in the air into one of several varieties of silk. Those strands used to support an orb web are smooth, not sticky, and one can run a finger along them without injury to the web. The snare, or inner part, on the other hand, is composed of silk which has drops of sticky material strung along it at regular intervals.

Spiders are variously colored. Some are bright yellow with black markings, others may be deep brown, striped, or distinguished by well marked patterns. The black widow spider is shiny black with hourglass-shaped markings of yellow, red, orange, or cream color on the underside.

Tarantulas are large, hairy spiders and are not, as many suppose, poisonous. Tiny mites, which may be red or other bright colors, are closely related to spiders.

Spiders differ from insects in that they have eight legs instead of six and only two parts to the body, a fused head and thorax (chest area), and an abdomen, whereas insects have three body parts. They have tiny eyespots arranged on the top of the forepart of the body, sometimes situated in a turretlike formation. Spiders with pearly-white eyes are night hunters.

WHERE TO FIND THEM

Look for spiders in shrubs, in the cracks of tree trunks, on window panes, in rooms where the window is not opened often, in the ground, in the corners of a room near the ceiling, or in places seldom exposed to light. The black widow is found only in dark places.

HOW TO KEEP THEM

Give spiders a large container so they will have the room in which to build their webs. The container should be closed with a screen top, or one that admits air. Except for jumping spiders they can be confined by means of a wide moat of water, such as a large baking pan with a flowerpot filled with soil in the center. In this two sticks can be anchored about 10-15 cm (4-6 inches) apart. In this kind of container a spider may build its web and the process can be watched.

WHAT TO FEED THEM

Spiders do not eat solid food. They suck the juices from insects and other small animals caught in their webs. Flies or small moths thrown into the web serve well as food. If confined, the spider must have water near at hand.

ACTIVITIES

1. Watch a spider build its web. This takes a long time to complete and it would be unwise to urge the children to stay beyond their interest span. They can always return from time to time.

2. Throw a fly into the web and observe how the spider shrouds it with silk which it manipulates with its legs. Later, if the spider is hungry it will insert its sharp mouthparts into the bundled-up victim. Otherwise, it will leave its prey hanging in the web for eating later.

3. Run a finger over the outer strand of silk of an orb spider's web and observe its smoothness; then try to run your finger over the other threads—you will find that they stick to your finger and destroy the web as you try to pull out.

4. Watch a spider escape by means of a dragline, which it carries around with it or emits very quickly as it evades danger. It will attach one end of the line to the place it is escaping from so quickly that the action is hard to detect.

5. Examine a spider web under a magnifying glass, paying particular attention to the various sorts of silk it is made of.

6. Look for a funnel web on the ground. These are made by wolf spiders which go out to hunt their prey instead of ensnaring them in a web. As they come and go from their hole in the ground they drag a silken line. This is what forms the funnel which grows larger and thicker in time.

7. The female wolf spider carries her young around on her back. Perhaps you will be lucky enough to come across one.

FUNNEL WEB

SHEET WEB

FORMLESS WEB

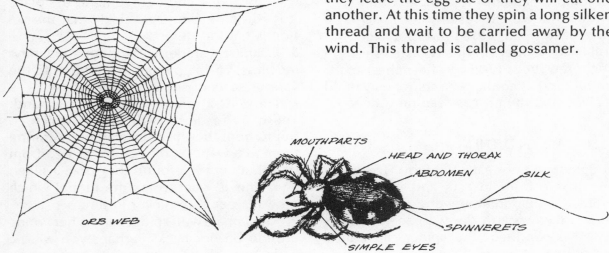

ORB WEB

8. Search for the garden spider which hides near its web, sometimes nearby underneath a leaf, sometimes within the web, and sometimes down a hole.

9. Examine a spider under a magnifying glass and locate its eyes and mouth. Notice the two organs at the front of the head. These, the chelicerae, are used to seize and kill prey. There is a tiny opening or a hook near the tip for the poison with which a spider stuns its victims so that they will remain quiet while they are being bundled up. There isn't enough poison nor is it virulent enough to harm a human (except in the black widow spider or other rare species known as brown spiders).

10. Look for the pearly, white egg sac made of heavy silk. If you can find one place it in a covered container and watch for the hatching spiderlings. Notice that they hatch in the same form as their parents and do not, like insects, go through a change of form.

11. The spiderlings must scatter soon after they leave the egg sac or they will eat one another. At this time they spin a long silken thread and wait to be carried away by the wind. This thread is called gossamer.

SOME HELPFUL MATERIALS

container, pans, etc.
covered jar
flowerpots
magnifying glasses
soil
sticks

KEY VOCABULARY FOR CHILDREN

black widow spider
cobwebs
garden spider
orbs
silk
snares
web
wolf spider

MOUTHPARTS
HEAD AND THORAX
ABDOMEN
SILK
SIMPLE EYES
SPINNERETS

Bibliography

FOR ADULTS

Bloome, Enid *The Water We Drink,* Garden City, N.Y., Doubleday & Co., Inc., 1971.

Comstock, John Henry *The Spider Book,* rev. ed., Ithaca, N.Y., Comstock Publishing Co., 1948.

David, Eugene *Spiders and How They Live,* Englewood Cliffs, N.J., Prentice-Hall, Inc., 1964.

Fabre, J. Henri *Life of the Spider,* New York, Horizon Press, 1971.

Gallant, Roy A. *Exploring the Weather,* Garden City, N.Y., Doubleday & Co., Inc. 1969.

Levi, Herbert W. and Lorna R. Levi *A Guide to Spiders and their Kin,* New York, Western Publishing Co., Inc., 1968.

Life (periodical) *Weather,* New York, Time-Life Books, 1965.

Naylor, Penelope *The Spider World,* New York, Franklin Watts Inc., 1973.

Nickelsburg, Janet *California Climates,* New York, Coward, McCann & Geoghegan, Inc., 1964.

Rothman, Joel *At Last to the Ocean: The Story of the Endless Cycle of Water,* New York, Macmillan, Inc., 1971.

Shuttlesworth, Dorothy E. *Story of Spiders,* Garden City, N.Y., Doubleday & Co., Inc., 1959.

FOR CHILDREN

Bartlett, Margaret F. *Where the Brook Begins,* New York, Thomas Y. Crowell Co., 1961.

Chenery, Janet *Wolfie,* New York, Harper & Row Publishers, Inc., 1969.

Dupre, Ramona Steward *Spiders,* Chicago, Follett Publishing Co., 1967.

Ets, Marie Hall *Gilberto and the Wind,* New York, Viking Press, Inc., 1963.

Goldin, Augusta R. *Spider Silk,* New York, Thomas Y. Crowell Co., 1964.

Graham, Margaret B. *Be Nice to Spiders,* New York, Harper & Row Publishers, Inc., 1967.

Green, Ivan *Splash and Tickle,* Fayetteville, Ga., Oddo Publishing Inc., 1968.

Huntington, Harriet E. *Let's Go to the Brook,* Garden City, N.Y., Doubleday & Co., Inc., 1952.

McDermott, Gerald *Anansi the Spider: A Tale from the Ashanti,* New York, Holt, Rinehart & Winston, Inc., 1972.

Milne, A. A. *Now We Are Six,* rev. ed., New York, E.P. Dutton & Co., Inc., 1961. "Waiting at the Window".

Shaw, Charles G. *It Looked Like Spilt Milk,* New York, Harper & Row Publishers, Inc., 1947.

Tresselt, Alvin *Follow The Wind,* New York, Lothrop, Lee and Shepard Co., 1950.

2 Projects with Small Animals

Grasshoppers, like all insects, have six legs and an outer skeleton (exoskeleton) of a rigid material called chitin. This is shed from time to time as the insect grows. The compound eyes of insects are composed of many six-sided lenses which give them a broken or mosaic picture of the world. For this reason their "feelers" (antennae) are their most important sense organs; grasshoppers have two antennae. The complicated mouthparts of grasshoppers are suitable for chewing tough grass. The brown "tobacco juice" grasshoppers spit out is nonpoisonous, though it has a bad smell and taste. This liquid helps protect the grasshopper from its enemies.

The pair of rear legs are much longer and stronger than the other four and enable the grasshopper to jump long distances. The forelegs, equipped with spines, are useful for climbing. A full-grown grasshopper has two pairs of wings. The upper two wings are horny and the lower two, which are thin and papery, fold away fanlike underneath the horny ones. The lower ones are sometimes brilliantly yellow and are used in flight.

Grasshoppers undergo an incomplete change of form (metamorphosis) in which the young resemble their parents when hatched but lack wings. Instead they have wingpads which enlarge with each molt, until the adult stage is reached and the wings at last become functional. Grasshoppers are usually green when the grasses are green and when the pastures and fields turn tawny they take on a tan coloration.

The sound a grasshopper produces comes from the legs or in some cases the wings, not from the mouth. The filelike edges of the rear legs are rubbed against the outer edge of the horny wings, or in some varieties the legs or the wings are rubbed against each other. Certain species of grasshoppers hear this sound by means of little, flat membranes, or hearing organs, situated just below the wings on the abdomen or rear part of the body. The female can be distinguished from the male by the presence of a long egg depositor (ovipositor) which extends from the rear of the abdomen.

You can tell a grasshopper from a cricket in the following way: the grasshopper's feelers (antennae) are shorter than its head (except in longhorn grasshoppers), which is placed at right angles to the body, the mouthparts facing the ground. Katydids and crickets have very long antennae and the cricket has two long appendages in the rear. The presence of a third appendage indicates a female, the extra one being the ovipositor. Crickets chirp at night and their wings are bent at a sharp angle to the sides of the body.

WHERE TO FIND THEM

Look for grasshoppers and crickets in the tall grass where they find shelter and food.

HOW TO CARE FOR THEM

Put them in a large covered bowl, terrarium, or jar. This should be amply stocked with fresh, green grasses or leaves which are renewed daily. No water is required.

If a terrarium is used cover the bottom with sod that has grass planted in it.

MALE CRICKET

FEMALE CRICKET

ACTIVITIES

1. Have a grasshopper hunt and catch them by means of a butterfly net.
2. Allow the children to hold them and to watch how they jump out of their hands. Estimate the distance and compare it with the distance the children can jump. (Be careful in holding the insects, as it is easy to tear off a leg).
3. Observe the grasshopper eating, to see how it chews off the food.
4. Watch a grasshopper climb up the stem of a piece of dry grass.
5. Observe a grasshopper through a magnifying glass. Locate the eyes with their six-sided lenses. This insect also has simple eyes, sensitive to light only, on the top of its head. See if you can find them.
6. If you can turn your grasshopper on its back and hold it there with a stick or a forceps, examine the mouth.

7. Look for the hearing membranes, or ears.
8. Note the legs, the rasp on the rear end, the strong muscular rear legs, and the weaker middle and fore pairs.
9. If you have found an immature grasshopper look for the wing pads. If the grasshopper is near the final molt you may even find the small wings peeping out below the pads.
10. You may find empty grasshopper skins. If so, look for the split down the back where the growing insect climbed out when it discarded the old skin.
11. Try a grasshopper race, watching carefully where the grasshoppers go. If they are already winged this will be difficult.
12. Draw or model grasshoppers.
13. Compose a grasshopper dance in which the children hop about.

SOME HELPFUL MATERIALS

butterfly nets
covered bowls, jars, or terrariums
crayons
drawing paper
magnifying glasses

KEY VOCABULARY FOR CHILDREN

*antennae
 crickets
 eyespots
 feelers
 katydids
*hearing membranes

*Suggested for older children only

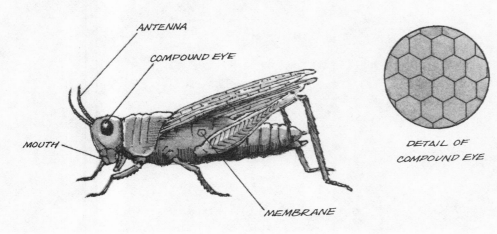

GRASSHOPPER

ANTENNA

COMPOUND EYE

MOUTH

MEMBRANE

DETAIL OF COMPOUND EYE

There are many varieties of caterpillars, as each species of moth or butterfly produces a different kind of caterpillar. Other insects produce larvae that resemble caterpillars, but the word *caterpillar* is applied only to the larvae of moths or butterflies.

Although caterpillars are of many shapes, colors, and sizes all have certain characteristics in common: All have three pairs of true legs, like the full-grown insect, which are attached to the section of the body behind the head (thorax). They also have from six to ten false legs (prolegs)—stubby, fleshy props on the rear part of the body (abdomen). Instead of the compound eyes of the adult insects the caterpillar has simple eyes on both sides of the head. It also has a pair of very short antennae.

The silk produced by caterpillars, unlike that of spiders, issues only from the mouth. In certain varieties of caterpillars the silk is spun into cocoons; in others it is used to build shelters. This is done by rolling or folding a leaf and fastening the edges together with the silk, after which the caterpillar creeps inside. Tent caterpillars incorporate whole branches and leaves into their shelter. Leaf miners chew their way into a leaf. One can follow their path by the clear outline on the surface of the leaf.

In time caterpillars go through a change (metamorphosis) in which they are transformed into pupae. Moth pupae are usually covered by a cocoon, while the pupae of butterflies form a chrysalis. The chrysalis is attached by the rear segment of the abdomen to a leaf or twig and the pupa

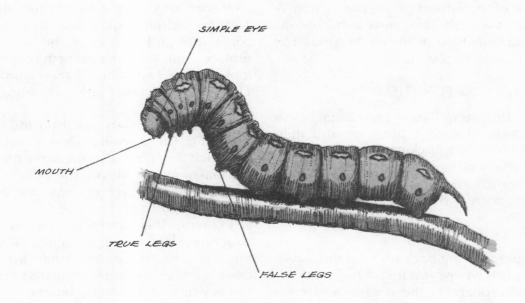

SIMPLE EYE

MOUTH

TRUE LEGS

FALSE LEGS

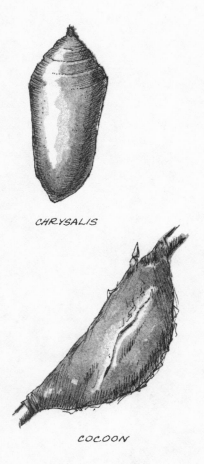

CHRYSALIS

COCOON

hangs head downwards during this period of development.

Cocoons are in some cases made entirely of silk and in others the silk is used to cement leaves, wood, or soil together, or as a glue in which the hairs that covered the caterpillar's body are embedded. Inside these cocoons and chrysalids (plural) the final metamorphosis takes place. The duration of the pupal state varies according to species and to the time of year, but eventually, unless the pupa has died, the winged insect emerges, gently waves its crumpled wings back and forth, pumping the veins full of liquid so that they become strong enough to support the weight of the insect in flight. When this happens the butterfly or moth takes flight.

WHERE TO FIND THEM

Look for a plant whose leaves are nibbled or show other signs of having been eaten. A caterpillar is most likely near at hand. You may also find one crawling on the ground or up the stems of plants.

HOW TO CARE FOR THEM

Place the caterpillars in a terrarium or in a cage made of wire netting, or of a milk carton and nylon stocking (see page 58). In any container there should be a twig or small branch for the insect to settle on to build its cocoon or chrysalis.

WHAT TO FEED THEM

Be sure to bring back some of the leaves of the plant where you found the caterpillar. In all probability, these leaves and these alone, are all it will eat. If you have found the caterpillar crawling along the ground or on a bare wall the insect was most likely looking for a spot to pupate and therefore will require no food at all. The leaves must be supplied daily, the excrement and dead or dry leaves removed. Be sure to replace the fresh leaves from the same species of plant from which you gathered the first ones. No water is needed because fresh leaves supply all the necessary moisture.

ACTIVITIES

1. The children should go on a caterpillar hunt, being sure to take along a container to carry the insect back. This container can be made of a milk carton with handles of string attached through holes in the sides.
2. Prepare a container for keeping the caterpillars. It is often better to have a container for each variety of caterpillar.
3. The children should help to clean the containers and to gather the leaves for replacement. When cleaning the container, look for the cast skins of the caterpillars. They shed their skin (molt) as they increase in size.
4. Let the caterpillars crawl on the hands and arms. These are harmless insects.
5. Watch the caterpillars eat along the edge of a leaf or make holes on the surface. They will often consume the whole leaf except for the tough veins.
6. Examine the caterpillar for its body structures: legs, prolegs, mouth, antennae, tiny eyespots. Some have other protective devices, such as large simulated eyes or horns which scare their enemies.

7. Observe a caterpillar under a magnifying glass to see the sharp spines on the true legs. These are used for holding objects and for clinging.

8. If you are fortunate you will catch a caterpillar in the act of attaching itself to a stick or twig and molting for the last time as it goes into pupation. With those caterpillars that spin cocoons you can watch the spinning but not the final molt, which takes place within the cocoon.

9. Watch, too, for the emerging winged insect from the chrysalis or cocoon. Remove the insect from its container and observe how it pumps the fluid into the crumpled wings until they expand to full size. Then take the butterfly or moth outside, release it, and watch it fly away.

10. Observe how the caterpillar walks—how it humps along, placing its legs on a surface, humping its body as it draws up the false legs, balancing on the false legs while once more extending its forelegs. Compare this to the locomotion of the earthworm (see pages 114–116). The children can imitate this form of locomotion on the floor and compose a caterpillar dance.

11. Caterpillars can be the models for drawings, paintings, and clay modeling.

SOME HELPFUL MATERIALS

jars or other containers
magnifying glasses
milk cartons and string
nylon stockings
terrarium containers

KEY VOCABULARY FOR CHILDREN

*chrysalis
 cocoon
 eyespots
 larva
 silk
 spines

*Suggested for older children only

Butterflies
and Moths

Because this book aims to introduce children to living creatures and not to museum specimens, netting butterflies or moths for the purpose of killing and impaling them is not recommended. Instead, this project will concern these insects as they are found outdoors or as they are temporarily caged, either because they have hatched from cocoons or chrysalids, or because they have been brought in to be observed, but not held in captivity for more than a few hours.

Butterflies and moths are insects and therefore have six legs, a pair of antennae, three parts to the body, and an outside skeleton that encloses the soft body parts. They go through a complete metamorphosis: from the egg a caterpillar hatches which sheds its skin as it grows, until it forms a pupa within a cocoon or chrysalis, later to emerge as an adult.

Both moths and butterflies have two pairs of wings that are hooked together in flight. In all but a few moths the forewings and hindwings differ both in shape and in veining. The wings are covered with scales that brush off like powder if handled. The mouth or sucking tube resembles a watch-spring rolled up tight underneath the head. When unrolled the tip is inserted into a flower and the nectar drawn up as through a straw.

You can differentiate between a moth and a butterfly by the shape of the antennae, which in butterflies have an elongated knob at the end. The antennae of moths lack this knob and may be variously formed, some being featherlike, others

BUTTERFLY

ANTENNA

HEAD

THORAX

ABDOMEN

MOTH

ANTENNA

HEAD

THORAX

ABDOMEN

with curved ends, and still others tapering to the point. Most moths fly at night while all butterflies are day fliers. When at rest most butterflies hold their wings erect above the body, while moths extend theirs parallel to the ground.

There are many sizes and colors of moths and butterflies and not all butterflies are beautiful nor are all moths dull in color.

WHERE TO FIND THEM

Clothes moths are tiny, brown, delicate insects. They are found in the house and are themselves harmless because they are unable to eat. It is the eggs they lay and the larvae that hatch from them that make them a menace, because the larvae eat wools and furs. Some moths are found near fruit trees, in places where grain is stored, and fluttering near leaves of oak trees, evergreen trees and shrubs, in vegetable gardens, and hovering around a light near an open window.

Look for butterflies near flowers, each type having its own preferences for the nectar of certain flowers. You can also frequently find butterflies drinking at a muddy spot. Butterflies can sometimes be attracted by placing a vase of brightly colored flowers outside or on the sill of an open window.

HOW TO CARE FOR THEM

If moths or butterflies are held for a short time, the container must be large enough that the insect will not tear its fluttering wings by beating them against the sides or top.

ACTIVITIES

1. Observe these insects in the field as they fly about or emerge from cocoons or chrysalids, which may be found hanging on the bark or twigs of trees and shrubs.

2. Watch a butterfly feed, as it unrolls its coiled mouth and sinks it into a flower.

3. Observe the veining of the wings and draw the children's attention to it when they draw pictures. The veins are the stiffening which give the wing strength. Compare the veins on several different kinds of butterflies and moths.

4. Observe the antennae of both moths and butterflies.

5. Notice the somewhat random flight of a butterfly and compare it to the purposeful flight of a bird.

6. Look for the large compound eyes on these insects. See if you can distinguish the six-sided lenses.

7. Look at the legs, count them, and see how a butterfly or moth uses them.

8. Notice the different pattern and shape of the forewing and the hindwing. See if you can find the ridge by which they are hooked together in flight.

9. Compare the coloring and pattern of one variety of moth with another, and of one variety of butterfly with another. Note the different patterns on the underside of the wings and the upper surface.

10. Draw pictures of each butterfly observed, trying to color accurately.

11. Compose a butterfly dance, trying to imitate the slow motion of a butterfly's wings.

SOME HELPFUL MATERIALS

magnifying glasses
terrarium container or
*   other large container*

KEY VOCABULARY FOR CHILDREN

adult
*antennae
*compound eyes
feelers
scales
veins

*Suggested for older children only

24

Bees

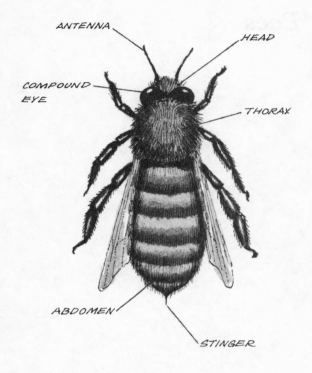

ANTENNA

HEAD

COMPOUND EYE

THORAX

ABDOMEN

STINGER

Bees, like all insects, have three body sections: head, thorax, and abdomen. On the head, in addition to the mouthparts, there are a pair of antennae and compound eyes composed of a multitude of six-sided lenses. Six jointed legs and the wings are attached to the thorax. Bees, like most insects, have two pairs of wings. At the rear of end of an insect's abdomen is an organ used for laying eggs, which in bees has been modified into a sting. The entire body is encased in a rigid, outside skeleton, which is shed from time to time as the bee increases in size.

There are a number of varieties of bees and as all of them can sting they cannot be handled. However, they can be observed outdoors. The large, yellow and black, fuzzy bumblebee is so occupied with looking for food for its young that it will not attack unless its nest underground is approached or it is actually molested. Bumblebees are not found in winter because they hibernate beneath the loose bark of trees or under logs. As soon as warm weather sets in the female comes out and begins to seek out a spot for her home. This may be in a deserted mouse nest, or an old bird's nest on the ground, or in a chamber underground, which she herself has dug. Once the nest is lined with leaves, the female bee goes out to stock her larder with pollen moistened with nectar gathered from flowers. The combination of these two ingredients produces honey for which she builds waxen pots. (The wax is secreted from her own body.) Some of the honey is left in piles on the ground and on these the eggs are laid. The larvae which hatch from the eggs are tiny, white grubs without eyes. The mother bumblebee feeds these until they spin themselves cocoons, then pupate, and finally emerge as winged adults. These now take over the feeding of their younger brothers and sisters by gathering pollen and nectar. The original female, or queen, continues to lay eggs until late summer. At that time a new generation of queens and males is produced. These leave the nest to mate, after which the male dies and the female digs in for her winter sleep.

All bees are hairy, even the shiny, brown honeybee. This variety builds a much more elaborate nest, or hive, in which to breed and care for their young. There are three types of honeybees, the queen or female, the drone or male, and the workers, also female. The workers tend the young, sweep out the vacant cells, constructed of wax, in which the eggs are laid. They also care for and feed the queen and the young in addition to foraging for food. Each of these jobs is taken on at a different period of their lives, the final one being devoted to gathering pollen which is packed into a cavity on the hind legs. This pollen, together with the nectar, which is sucked up by a long tongue inserted into the flowers, is brought back to the hive to be converted into honey or beeswax.

WHERE TO FIND THEM

Look for bees near flowers in bloom, in a field of clover, or in a clump of flowering sage bushes.

HOW TO CARE FOR THEM

It would be rather difficult to maintain a hive, but it is possible to visit an apiary where honey is produced, or some natural history museum which may have live hives installed. Here the bees enter the hives through a glass tube, and a cover of one side of the hive may be of glass.

ACTIVITIES

1. Watch a bee settle on a flower. You can move up quietly without disturbing the bee. You can then observe the bee as it sinks its tongue into the flower for nectar and as it packs the pollen into the pollen baskets on the rear legs.

2. Follow a bumblebee (at a distance) to where it goes underground. Then wait for it to come out. In this way you will discover where it nests.

3. A bumblebee could be kept for a short time under a glass tumbler, and the large compound eyes and tiny eyespots between them observed. Notice too the manner in which the antennae are used as feelers.

4. While the bee is under the glass look for the pollen baskets on the legs and notice the comb, also on the legs, used to rake the pollen from the hairy body.

BECAUSE ACTIVITIES 5 AND 6 REQUIRE A GOOD DEAL OF INACTIVE WATCHING, THEY ARE BEST SUITED FOR OLDER CHILDREN.

5. Notice the thin, papery wings, their veining, and where they are attached to the body. Count the wings.

6. Observe the three parts to the body and see if you can locate the stinger.

7. If possible visit a place where honeybees are kept. If possible view an active honeycomb through glass or when handled by a skilled beekeeper.

8. Obtain honey in the comb, usually available at country-type markets. Let the children break the comb and taste the honey, perhaps spreading some honey and beeswax (which is edible) on fresh bread.

SOME HELPFUL MATERIALS

magnifying glasses
tumblers or jars

KEY VOCABULARY FOR CHILDREN

adults
bumblebee
*drone
hive
honey
honeybee
honeycomb
*pollen
queen
wax
*worker

Suggested for older children only

Ladybird
Beetles

Ladybird, Ladybird, fly away home,
        Your house is on fire, your children are burning!

The story connected with this nursery rhyme runs like this: The ladybird beetle was found on the hop vines in England. These vines were burned every year after the hops were picked. Because the ladybird beetles ate the aphids which destroyed the vines, people used to sing them this ditty to warn the beetles to save themselves from being burned. Because they assisted the farmer to rid his plants of pest, they were called Beetles of Our Lady, a gift from the Virgin Mary, and from that, ladybird beetles.

A beetle is an insect with two pairs of wings, the outer pair being tough and horny and meeting in a straight line down the middle of the back. The inner pair, which is thin and papery, folds away beneath the other pair and supports the beetle in flight. Like other insects, beetles have three parts to the body, a head, thorax, and abdomen. On the head are a pair of antennae, the compound eyes made up of small, hexagonal lenses, and the mouthparts suitable for chewing. On the thorax are six legs and two pairs of wings. On the abdomen are the breathing holes (spiracles) and in females at the rear end is the egg-laying organ (ovipositor).

There are many species of beetles, large and small; some are found on the ground, others in the bark of trees, and still others in the water. Some have long antennae, some are black or brown, and some a beautiful iridescent color.

The ladybird beetle, like most insects, goes through metamorphosis. When it hatches from the egg, the larva has pincers on the head and a flat body, and only after metamorphosis does it take on its typical form and color.

Both the larva and adult ladybird beetle are considered beneficial by gardeners because they feed on aphids, which are very destructive to roses and other garden plants.

In the winter the ladybird beetle either crawls into a hole to hibernate or congregates with others in a great mound, climbing one on top of another for the same purpose.

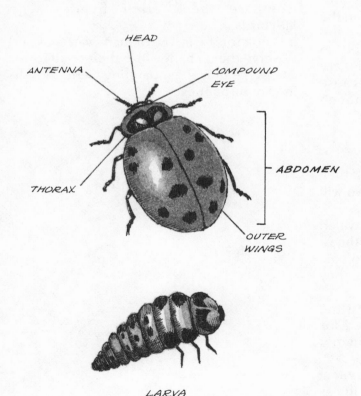

LARVA

WHERE TO FIND THEM

Look for them on any shrub that is infested with aphids. They are especially common on unsprayed rose bushes.

HOW TO KEEP THEM

Place a thin layer of soil at the bottom of a large glass jar or terrarium and keep it fairly moist but not wet. Provide a place for the insects to hide; a twig or a small stone lying on the soil will serve this purpose.

WHAT TO FEED THEM

Feed them aphids. Cut a branch from the infested bush on which you found the ladybird or any other and continue to provide plenty of food, for these beetles are heavy feeders. No water is needed because the bodies of the aphids contain enough liquid.

ACTIVITIES

1. The children should gather them. If they cannot find a large number, one or two will suffice to start the project.
2. Turn them over on their backs and watch them "play dead" and later right themselves. See which legs they use to do so.
3. Try to feed them grass or leaves—they will not take such food.
4. Observe through a magnifying glass the shape of the mouth, which is formed for piercing and sucking in the ladybird and not for chewing as in many other beetles.
5. Take a good look at the aphids too! Most of them are wingless and suck the juices from plants. They deposit a sticky liquid, called honeydew, relished not only by ladybird beetles but by ants as well.
6. Provoke a ladybird beetle to flight and watch it unfold its papery wings from underneath the outer horny ones. Follow the flying insect to where it lands and observe how the inner wings are folded away.
7. The children should handle these insects and have them crawl over their hands.
8. Collect other varieties of beetles, such as click-beetles (which rub the thorax and abdomen together, producing a click) iridescent scarabs, and wood-borers. Compare these other beetles with ladybirds.
9. Look for the larvae of many varieties and observe them change into their adult form.
10. Make drawings, paintings, and models in clay of beetles.

SOME HELPFUL MATERIALS

magnifying glasses
plants with aphids
soil
terrarium container or large jar
twigs

KEY VOCABULARY FOR CHILDREN

adult
aphid
feelers
larva
papery wings

THIS IS A PROJECT BETTER SUITED TO OLDER CHILDREN IN THAT IT IS ONE THAT REQUIRES QUIET EXAMINATION AND HAS LITTLE ACTIVE PARTICIPATION CONNECTED WITH THE ACTIVITIES.

A fly is an insect and therefore has three body parts: head, thorax, and abdomen, and an exoskeleton which covers its body. The organs are attached to the inner surface of the exoskeleton. A fly also has six legs and a pair of antennae. Its mouth is used for sucking and lapping, because a fly subsists only on liquids. Unlike other insects a fly has only two wings, the rear ones being replaced by a pair of rods with knobs at the end. These rods, called halteres (*hal*-ter-eeze), twirl in flight and serve to stabilize the insect much as a gyroscope stablizes a vessel at sea.

Flies go through a complete metamorphosis. From eggs hatch legless larvae, called maggots, which seek out dark places in which they grow at a tremendous rate for six days. Pupation begins when the outer skin hardens into a brown cylindrical case inside of which the maggot turns into a fly. After about a week it emerges and reaches maturity in three days. It starts to lay eggs right away and continues to do so for a period of two months, for this is the life span of most flies.

Flies have large, compound eyes that take up the major part of the head, even extending around the sides and to the rear. Thus the insect can see in almost every directtion. But it is the sense of smell that directs a fly to its food. The organ of smell is in the antennae and the taste organ is in the feet.

The feet are equipped with tiny claws and hairy pads on the under side, which produce a sticky fluid that enables a fly to walk upside down on the ceiling.

The mouth of the housefly is adapted for sponging and lapping. It is composed of a flat pad suspended from the lower part of the head and is provided with channels into which saliva can run.

The humming noise made by flies is made by the rapid beat of the wings.

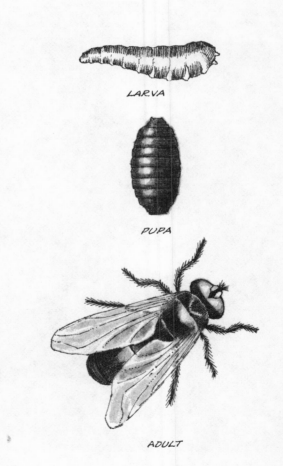

LARVA

PUPA

ADULT

WHERE TO FIND THEM

Look for flies on a window pane or buzzing around exposed sweets or other foods. If fruit is placed outdoors in a shallow dish it will attract flies. Trap them by placing a glass or plastic jar over them.

HOW TO KEEP THEM

Place them in a transparent container with a tight screen top so the flies cannot escape.

WHAT TO FEED THEM

Place a lump of sugar or a bit of meat in the container.

ACTIVITIES

The children should not handle the flies. They carry disease and should be studied only in their container.

1. Look for the compound eyes. Study them through a magnifying glass and see if the children can observe the many six-sided lenses of which they are composed.

2. Notice the shape of the mouth and watch a fly eating.

3. Using a magnifying glass study the antennae and notice that they are segmented. Also look at the feet and see if you can find the pads on the lower surface.

4. If you have caught a female fly you may find eggs in your container. Keep these and watch them become maggots, develop into pupae, and finally into winged flies.

5. Look at the wings and note the pattern of the veins and how it differs from that of grasshoppers, moths, and butterflies.

6. Look for the halteres and if the fly is in motion see if you can watch them spinning. (This is almost impossible to see, as they spin so fast, but try it anyway.)

7. Watch a fly cleaning itself with its front feet. The routine starts with the fly using the tiny hairs and claws on one foot to scrape and brush the other foot. Next the fly cleans its head and last the other two pairs of legs.

8. You may also catch other species of flies, such as the fat blue bottles, crane flies, bee flies, and many others. All flies can best be distinguished from bees by their having only two wings. Gnats and mosquitos also belong to the same group as flies, the Diptera, or two-winged insects. If you do find other members of the Diptera, compare the mouthparts, for these insects can often be distinguished from one another by the shape of the mouth.

SOME HELPFUL MATERIALS

container, transparent, with
  screen top
fruit, meat, and sugar lumps
jars, clear glass or plastic
magnifying glasses

KEY VOCABULARY FOR CHILDREN

*abdomen
*compound eyes
*halteres
  larvae
*thorax
*veins

*Suggested for older children only

Tadpoles, Frogs and Toads

Frogs and toads are amphibians, a word meaning "two lives". During their larval state most amphibians live entirely in the water, where they breathe by means of gills. When fully grown they breathe air by means of lungs.

Tadpoles, or pollywogs, the larval form of toads and frogs, are found in the early spring in mud puddles, shallow ponds, and brooks. The eggs from which they recently hatched were covered with a colorless jelly. The eggs of toads are arranged in long strings while frogs' eggs are in a tight cluster.

After hatching the tiny tadpole remains attached to the egg yolk while completing its development. Before long the tadpole begins to swim about and to eat by scraping its small mouth along the surface of a submerged leaf, where algae grow. The tadpole is herbivorous, meaning that it feeds entirely on vegetation. In time the hind legs begin to grow, and if you observe closely you can note that the tail is gradually becoming smaller as it is absorbed. The forelegs appear later and when they have grown to full size the tail will be gone. While these visible changes are taking place internal ones are also occurring: The digestive tract changes in such a way that the herbivorous diet has to be abandoned for a carnivorous (meat-eating) one; the gills are replaced by lungs. During the time these structures are developing the tadpoles can be observed coming to the surface of the water to gulp dry air and to expand the growing lungs.

When metamorphosis is complete, the toad or frog is ready to leave its early environment and to take up its existence on land. Here it remains until the time arrives when it returns to the water, mates, and lays eggs.

Toads and frogs can be distinguished one from the other by a number of characteristics: A toad's skin is dry and "warty", while that of a frog is moist and smooth. (Note that the "warts" on a toad's skin bear no relation to those which sometimes grow on our own skin. Because these so-called warts are not contagious, toads can be freely handled). Both frogs and toads periodically shed their skin, which serves not only as a covering but also as an auxiliary to the lungs. The porous, moist skin can admit air and thus assist in the process of breathing, as do also the muscles of the throat.

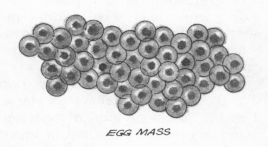

EGG MASS

TADPOLE

ADULT FROG

The toad's head is broader at the tip than the frog's, which tapers distinctly. The flat membrane on each side of the head, marking the external ear, is smaller on the toad than in the frog. The toad is nocturnal; the frog feeds by day.

In both amphibians the tongue is attached to the front of the inner surface of the mouth. This enables them to thrust the long, sticky organ out and to flick back their prey with lightning speed and thus to pick up their food on the wing.

The forelegs, with only four toes, are much shorter than the rear ones. In order to hold a frog or toad securely one must grip the hind legs to prevent the animal from hopping away.

WHERE TO FIND THEM

Frogs are found in damp places in or near water, while toads live in drier places. Because of their nocturnal habits toads are somewhat harder to find than frogs because they hide away by day.

Look for tadpoles in the early spring in shallow bodies of water. When you scoop them up, take along some of the water you found them in and put it in your aquarium, as it contains algae, the food of tadpoles.

HOW TO CARE FOR THEM

You can keep tadpoles in most aquariums or fish bowls. Clean the container about once a week. As soon as the pollywogs have developed four legs, drain all but a scant inch of water and place a flat rock with a gradually sloping edge in the aquarium so that the animals can climb out of the water.

Frogs and toads must be placed in a covered container, or they will hop out. A large terrarium is suitable and can be planted with ferns, grasses, and other small plants. It should contain a bowl of water large enough for the amphibians to climb into.

WHAT TO FEED THEM

If the aquarium is placed in direct sunlight the green algae that grow on the inside of the glass will make suitable food for the tadpoles. This food can be supplemented with chicken mash, egg yolks, bits of liver sausage or other lunch meet, cooked oatmeal or packaged fish food—but not all at the same time. Lettuce leaves broken into fine bits are suitable too.

As frogs and toads are carnivorous they can be fed insects, spiders, slugs, caterpillars, centipedes, termites, and other small animals. Because of their poor eyesight these amphibians can only spot moving prey, so if live food cannot be procured, bits of raw meat, cheese, or fish wriggled up and down can be substituted. These should be placed on the tip of a spoon, or on a toothpick or broomstraw and moved up and down before the animal's eyes.

ACTIVITIES

1. Go out in the springtime to catch tadpoles with nets and a container that can hold water. It would be well to scout the possible spots before taking the children, lest they fail to find these animals.
2. Prepare the aquarium and later the terrarium for the full-grown animals.

3. Watch the day-by-day changes of the metamorphosing tadpoles—the growth of the hind legs and later of the forelegs and the gradual absorption of the tail.

4. Watch how the tadpole breathes and compare this with the breathing of a fish. Also notice the difference in the way the tadpole and fish swim.

5. Observe the very small mouth of the tadpole and compare its shape with that of a fish.

6. Go on a frog or toad hunt with a long-handled net.

7. Feed the frogs and keep their container watered so that the plants in the terrarium will not die. Change the water in the container periodically.

8. Observe the throat of the frog or toad and note how the muscles assist the somewhat rudimentary lungs to breathe.

9. Look for the flat ears on the sides of the head.

10. Observe the feet—the difference between the rear and front ones, the pads on the underside of the forelegs of the male, and the number of toes on both feet.

11. Draw pictures or make models in clay. The change of the tadpole to frog or toad might suggest a series of pictures which might later be assembled into a book.

12. Let the children imitate the hopping and compose a frog dance. If your frogs have croaked, the sound effects could be added.

13. A frog race might be attempted, each group having its own frog to compete. This should cause much exasperation or merriment when the animal refuses to cooperate and to stay on the race course.

SOME HELPFUL MATERIALS

aquarium or other container, covered
bowl
egg yolks
fish food
liver sausage
nets, long handled
oatmeal, cooked
rocks, flat
spoons
toothpicks, or broomstraws

KEY VOCABULARY FOR CHILDREN

*ear membrane
 gills
 lungs

*Suggested for older children only

Daddy Longlegs

THIS PROJECT IS SUITABLE FOR OLDER CHILDREN IN THAT IT LACKS A GREAT DEAL OF ACTIVE PARTICIPATION.

There are two species that are known by the name of daddy longlegs, though they are only distantly related. One is the harvestman spider and the other is the crane fly. You can tell them apart if you count the legs, as the harvestman spider has eight and the crane fly six. The crane fly, as with all flies, has three parts to its body, one pair of wings and a pair of rods with ball-shaped objects at the end, the halteres, instead of the second pair of wings. The harvestman spider has no wings, and its body has only two parts, which are joined together to form a single unit. Both these animals (only the crane fly is an insect) have long spindly legs which break off if roughly handled.

Though the *harvestman* belongs in the spider group it is actually quite different from other spiders. Its body is not composed of two parts, it does not spin a web, and its organs for grasping (on the head) are quite different in shape. It has been given the name harvestman because it is most often seen at harvest time. The adults hide away in the daytime but come out at twilight to search for food. It is then that they come into our homes and barns and light on the bark of trees, sometimes in great numbers.

Harvestman eggs are laid in the ground and do not hatch until the next spring. When the young hatch they are white in color with only the black eyes shining out of their turret on the top of the body, one looking in each lateral direction.

Harvestmen feed mostly on dead animals, though it is said that in captivity they will eat soft vegetables and fruit as well as aphids.

When walking the harvestman's legs are bent in the middle and the body is suspended not far off the ground. When the spider is disturbed, the second pair is waved around, as the animal balances on the other three pairs of legs, as though it were trying to locate danger. Most harvestmen die when winter comes and are replaced by the young which hatch from over-wintering eggs.

The *crane fly* goes through metamorphosis. The larvae hatch from eggs laid in very damp soil. Wormlike in form, these larvae feed mostly on decaying vegetable matter. Some will eat living plants, though, and one variety is a serious pest on wheat.

After almost a year the larvae go into pupation in damp, even wet, oozy mud, to emerge twelve days later as large, winged insects.

The crane fly is entirely harmless, as its mouth is formed in such a way that it can neither suck or pierce.

Its halteres are easily seen even without the use of magnification, but the antennae should be observed with a magnifying glass so that the male can be distinguished from the female. The male antennae are long and feathery or saw-toothed while the female's are thin and threadlike.

WHERE TO FIND THEM

Harvestmen and crane flies are found flying around or stalking on the walls, especially in the fall.

HARVESTMAN

CRANE FLY

WHAT TO DO WITH THEM

Observe them where they are. Do not try to pick them up or they will be crushed, especially the crane flies. If a glass tumbler is placed over one or the other they can be observed through the transparent glass.

ACTIVITIES

1. Compare the harvestman with the crane fly, pointing out the different body parts and behavior of each species.

2. Look for the eyes on top of the harvestman's body and the compound eyes on the head of the crane fly.

3. Compare the manner in which each animal walks.

4. Notice the absence of wings on the harvestman.

5. Look for the veins on the wings of the crane fly, and compare them with those of other insects. Also observe the halteres.

6. A female cranefly, in addition to the distinguishing antennae, has an ovipositer at the rear of her body. Look for it.

7. Watch the actions of the harvestman when disturbed—how it uses its legs to locate danger.

SOME HELPFUL MATERIALS

magnifying glasses
tumblers or jars, clear

KEY VOCABULARY FOR CHILDREN

*antennae
  feelers
*halteres
  larvae

*Suggested for older children only

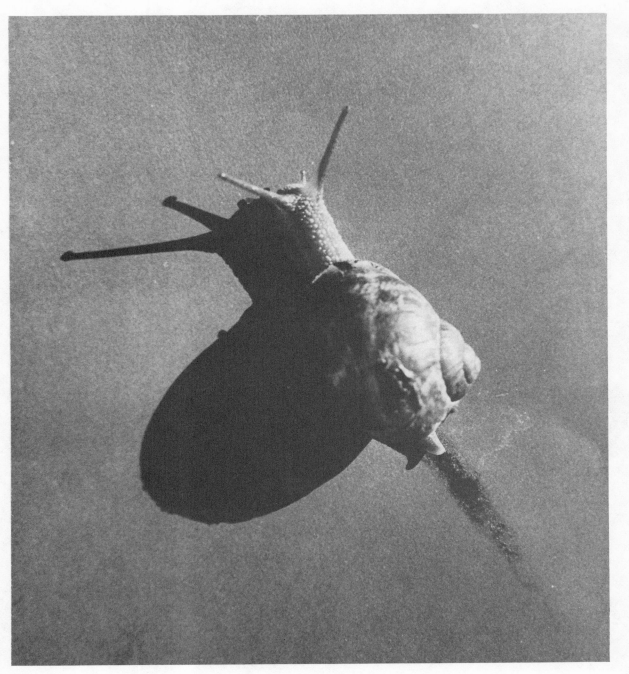

Snails and slugs belong to that group of animals known as mollusks, which are soft-bodied and without backbones. In this group are included not only land snails and slugs and sea snails but shellfish such as clams and oysters, mussels, scallops, limpets, and abalones.

Inside of the shell of the mollusk, covering the soft body parts, is the mantle whose function it is to secrete the shell. Material is added around the open mouth of the shell, ever widening the spiral.

The organ of locomotion is a fleshy, muscular foot that can be extended and withdrawn into the shell. The foot secretes a slimy mucus which enables the snail or slug to glide along without losing the moisture in the body. Slugs are similar to snails but have no outer shell. Their entire bodies are covered with this slimy mucus.

On the head of the snail or slug are two pairs of tentacles. On the tip of each of the longer ones is a dark spot, the eye, by which the animal can only distinguish light from dark. The shorter pair of tentacles is said to contain the organ of smell. Within the mouth is a ribbonlike organ called the radula, with its horny row of teeth turned backward into the mouth. By means of the radula the slug or snail rasps off food from the edges of leaves and other soft plant materials, as slugs and land snails are herbivorous animals.

The pulsating hole on the side of the body is the opening into the breathing organ, or lungs.

WHERE TO FIND THEM

Land snails are not common in some areas east of the Mississippi. Slugs, on the other hand, can be found throughout the United States. Snails are mostly found in damp spots where plants are growing, though some can be picked up at the seashore. Slugs usually stay under leaves, boards, or rocks. Some snails can be purchased at fish markets in the east, if none are found outdoors. These are large and very active, making them easy to observe.

HOW TO KEEP THEM

Gather only three or four snails or slugs to a large glass. If too many are confined in a small area they will cover one another with mucus and form a tight ball. These animals can also be kept in a planted terrarium, though they may destroy the plants by eating them.

WHAT TO FEED THEM

Lettuce, celery tops, spinach, or any leaves containing plenty of moisture. Replenish the food frequently and keep the container clean. No water is needed if the leaves are sufficiently moist.

ACTIVITIES

1. The children can collect the snails themselves. Slugs, because of their coat of mucus, are less appealing and probably best observed outdoors. In searching for them observe the trail of dried mucus, looking like a silver ribbon, which the snail or slug has laid down.

SNAIL

SLUG

2. The children can feed the snails and keep the container free of old dried-out leaves.

3. Place snails or slugs on a piece of black construction paper and notice the silvery trail they lay down. This will dry into interesting patterns, which last about a week and then peel away from the paper. The mucus is in no way harmful and if some is picked up on the hands it can be washed off in running water. Each child might have his own snail and paper and the patterns made by the moving snail might be compared.

4. Place the snails on a pane of glass and observe both from above and below the way the foot is used in locomotion. SAFETY NOTE: *Be sure that sharp edges of the glass are covered with tape.*

5. Notice the two pairs of tentacles and look for the black spots on the tips of the longer pair. As these eyes are sensitive only to light, they might be shaded from the source of light by a piece of paper or the hand. Then watch the snail or slug withdraw the tentacles. Notice that they are actually turned inside out like the fingers of a glove. Once the animal is no longer afraid, the tentacles will be poked out again.

6. Look for the opening on the right side of the body and watch it pulsate as the animal breathes. Let the children compare this with their own breathing and the rise and fall of the chest. To prove that this opening is not the mouth, have the children place food close to it.

7. The mouth is located on the underside of the snail just behind the second pair of tentacles. Place a piece of succulent lettuce or other food close to the snail's mouth and observe the manner in which it eats. If you can watch this from below you may see the radula within the mouth and how it is used.

8. Turn the snail over on its back and watch how it regains its normal upright position.

9. The children might pretend they are snails, moving along the floor by gliding and using their fingers to show how a snail eats and how it rights itself by turning over.

10. Collect snail shells and compare them with the shells of sea snails, such as turban shells, conches, periwinkles, and cowries.

11. Look for snail eggs underneath leaf mold. They are chalky white and the size of small pearls. Keep them in a damp spot underneath leafmold until they hatch. The tiny snails can be kept and their growth watched.

SOME HELPFUL MATERIALS

container, large, glass
construction paper, black
glass pane, taped edges
leaves, fresh green
terrarium with plants

KEY VOCABULARY FOR CHILDREN

mucus
shell
*tentacles
trail

*Suggested for older children only

Lizards

Lizards are reptiles and are cold-blooded, taking on the temperature of their environment. Unlike amphibians they are usually able to live in dry places because of their thick, scaly skin which prevents the loss of vital body fluids. Their eggs have a leathery shell which also serves to hold in moisture. Newborn reptiles, though smaller, resemble their parents and do not go through a metamorphosis.

Most lizards have four legs, each with five toes tipped with claws. (Amphibians have only four toes on the front feet.) All but a few lizards can blink their eyes because, unlike snakes, they have moveable eyelids. Their ears are well developed and can be observed as a pair of flat membranes or holes, one on each side of the head.

While most lizards lay their eggs on the ground in cracks of rocks, some, such as the alligator lizard, retain their eggs in their body until they hatch. Although this type of reptile seems to bear live young, like mammals, the embryo is enclosed in a shell.

Lizards can be safely handled, though they will nip and pinch with their jaws if frightened. The only poisonous lizard is the Gila monster, which lives in the desert and even this one is so slow moving that it is not much of a menace.

One sometimes comes across a lizard without a tail or with a short, stubby, regenerated one, because when attacked the lizard can shed its tail. The tail will continue to wriggle as the lizard itself escapes from its assailant.

Like the snake, also a reptile, the lizard sheds its skin from time to time, sometimes all in one piece and at other times torn to shreds.

WHERE TO FIND THEM

Look for lizards in a warm spot, such as on a boulder or log in the sunshine. However, a lizard will hide in the shade if the spot becomes too hot. Then it is found underneath logs, boards, rocks or in leaf piles. A desert lizard prefers open spaces, however.

HOW TO CATCH A LIZARD

Make a noose from thread or fish line and attach it to a pole. Approach the lizard slowly and quietly so that your shadow does not precede you and slip the noose over the lizards's head. (Another way to catch a lizard is to let the children do it. They are often so quick that they can pick it up in their hands.)

HOW TO CARE FOR THEM

Place a lizard in a terrarium with a screened lid, with glass on one side and wood or other opaque material on the other sides. If screening is used the reptile may injure itself by rubbing up against it. Cover the floor of the terrarium with dry sand or gravel and place a large piece of bark in the container for a shelter. In cold weather a 75-100 watt lightbulb will warm the cage sufficiently so that the animal will not stop eating and drinking and die. If kept in a planted terrarium the lizard will obtain enough water from a daily sprinkling of the plants. Otherwise place a container with water in the cage.

WHAT TO FEED THEM

The water dish in the cage must be kept filled with fresh, clean water. If the lizard refuses to drink, hold its head under water for a moment and when it begins to swallow free it. Lizards eat mealworms, centipedes, spiders, sowbugs, earthworms, flies, grasshoppers, etc. It is sometimes difficult to get a lizard in captivity to eat. If this becomes impossible let the lizard go and try to replace it with one that will eat. Feed sparingly twice a week.

ACTIVITIES

1. Compare the lizard with a salamander (see pages 47–49). Notice the difference in skin texture. Feel the lizard and you will be able to feel the rough scales. On some lizards these are sharp-pointed and on others smooth. Compare the feet and the method of getting about.

2. Notice that the scales on the undersurface of the animal differ from those on the back.

3. Observe how a lizard can close its eyes and note the action of the eyelids.

4. Locate the ears on the side of the head.

5. Look inside the lizard's mouth by provoking it to open the mouth and inserting the side of a pencil between the jaws.

6. If you have found a couple of blue bellies (Fence Lizards), you can distinguish the male from the female by the male's brighter coloring. If you have two males you may note the manner in which they display their blue markings to each other. In this way they establish their own territorial rights and frighten away intruders.

7. Horned toads, which are rightly lizards and not toads, may be brought in from the desert or can sometimes be purchased. These reptiles have sharp spines on the body and horns on the head. They must be kept in a dry cage that is warmed in cold weather.

8. Tie a string around the body of your lizard and set it free in the room or open space outside and observe how it moves.

9. You may become the possessor of a chameleon too. This slender lizard, whose body is colored a golden green above and white below, often has a reddish, pendant fold of skin below the jaw. Don't expect the chameleon to flash color changes, for it will change color only with temperature changes or when excited. When cold it becomes a dull grey, when warm a light green, and when frightened the colors fade, while in full sunshine it looks dull black and at night cream colored. A chameleon requires warmth at all times and should be sprinkled with water from time to time as it obtains its water from dew drops in nature.

10. If you have more than one variety of lizard, compare them.

11. Make drawings, paintings, and models of the lizards.

12. You might plan to return to this project some time in the future for there are a number of different kinds of lizards that display different qualities and behavior.

SOME HELPFUL MATERIALS

pieces of bark
bulb, 75 watt, in lamp socket
dish, shallow
sand or gravel, dry
terrarium with screened lid
wood pieces

KEY VOCABULARY FOR CHILDREN

cold-blooded
horns
reptile
scaly skin
spines

Salamanders are amphibians and, as they are cold blooded, they take on the temperature of the surroundings. They also go through a metamorphosis. When they hatch from eggs as larvae most species breathe through gills and many are therefore aquatic. Only after metamorphosis do they aquire lungs. Like other amphibians salamanders have a naked, scaleless, moist skin, which assists the lungs in bringing air into the body, but by the same token cannot prevent moisture inside the body from escaping. That is why a salamander requires a damp spot in which to live. Frogs and toads are tailless amphibians. The salamander alone possesses a tail it can shed without serious consequences when fleeing from an enemy. A new tail will later grow in its place.

The salamander has no visible ears. Sound reaches the inner ear as vibrations transmitted by special muscles in the forelimbs. Apparently communication between individuals is limited because the only sound the salamander is capable of producing is a tiny squeak.

Some varieties of salamanders go through what corresponds to metamorphosis, emerging from the egg in a form unlike that of their parents. These salamanders hatch from eggs laid in damp spots on land.

Others, which spend their larval state in the water, have feathery gills that stand out from both sides of the head. Some of these salamanders may have fins on their ventral and dorsal surfaces. Only later do the lungs and limbs develop.

Aquatic salamanders lay their eggs encased in strings of a clear jellylike substance which is attached to such objects as twigs extending into the water.

All land salamanders are secretive and live in dark, moist spots in or near a source of water. They feed by night and the larvae are carnivorous.

WHERE TO FIND THEM

Look for salamanders underneath large rocks that are not too firmly embedded in the soil or underneath logs or boards. Newts, one variety of salamander, are found in slow-moving streams or shallow pools or ditches. Still others are found in wet meadows, fields, or even damp cellars. Eastern newts live on land for years, then return to water. During this land stage they are orange in color and are called red efts. Red efts are easily found in the woods beneath moist leaves.

LARVAL SALAMANDER SHOWING
GILLS FOR WATER HABITAT

HOW TO KEEP THEM

Keep salamanders in a container with a couple of inches of damp—not wet—soil on its floor. They can also be kept in a planted terrarium. A board or rock should be placed in the container for the salamander to creep under. Newts and other aquatic salamanders must have a shallow pan of water large enough for them to climb into. Cover the container to exclude excessive light. Salamander eggs can only be placed in an aquarium having an air pump. After they hatch and the larvae begin to change form, there must be a place from which they can climb out onto dry land.

WHAT TO FEED THEM

Salamanders are carnivorous. Stock your terrarium with earthworms which may burrow underground but will nevertheless be found by the salamanders. Beetles or other insects, snails, sowbugs, mealworms, or bits of raw meat are suitable food. To feed the meat dangle it on a broomstraw or thread before the salamander's eyes. (The presence of sowbugs in the container may keep the salamanders from becoming sluggish).

ACTIVITIES

1. Because the skin of these amphibians must remain moist they cannot be handled too much. However, none of them are poisonous, and the child should have the opportunity to pick them up in order to find out what they feel like. Hands should be thoroughly washed afterwards.

2. If the tail is shed during handling, reassure the child that it will grow again and watch the stub from time to time to see this regeneration.

3. Experiment with feeding the salamanders to see which food they will take.

4. If you dig your captive salamander out from under a rock or board, be sure to return it to a similar spot when you have finished with your observations. If it dries out it will die.

5. Watch how the salamander walks, how it is unable to lift its body far off the ground as its legs will not support its weight.

6. Compare a salamander with a lizard. Notice the difference in skin texture, the scales of the lizard and smooth surface of the salamander, the dry lizard skin and the moist salamander skin. Notice the difference in the feet and "hands" and count the number of fingers on both animals.

7. Observe the eyes of salamanders living under rocks. Their prominence enables them to see better in dark places.

8. Try to find a string of salamander eggs and to hatch them in an aquarium. This may take a long time, so don't be impatient!

9. Examine the eggs through a magnifying glass and see if you can discern the embryo inside. It is dark in color and after the first few days shaped like a comma. It is difficult to raise these animals in captivity as they require running water.

10. Notice the auxiliary muscles in the throat. These assist the lungs in breathing.

12. Have the children imitate the locomotion of the salamander and compare this to the way a lizard can scurry about.

SOME HELPFUL MATERIALS

aquarium with aerator
containers, clear, plastic
   or glass
pan, small
rock or small board
terrarium with plants

KEY VOCABULARY FOR CHILDREN

*amphibians
 cold-blooded
*embryo
 gills
 larvae
 newts
 red efts

*Suggested for older children only

Turtles

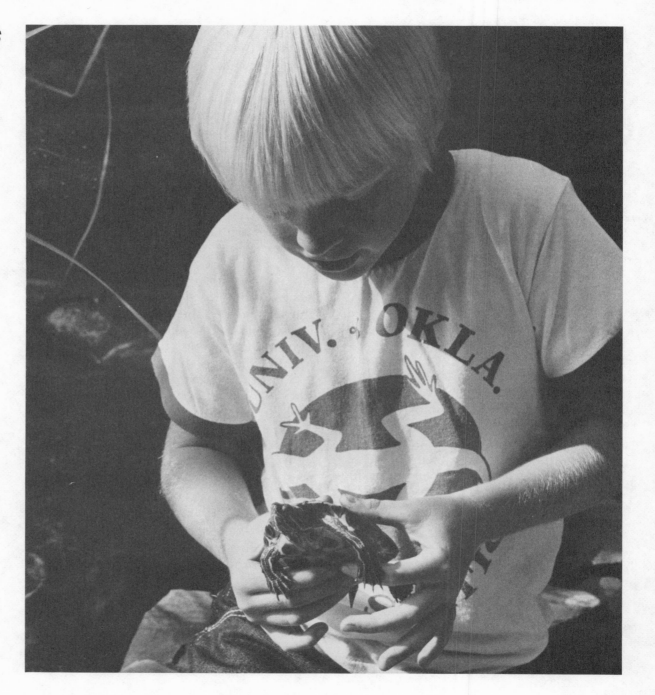

A turtle is a reptile and is therefore cold-blooded, meaning that it takes on the temperature of its surroundings. The skin of the reptile, unlike that of an amphibian, is dry and scaly and so constituted that it is impervious to moisture from without and also capable of containing the bodily moisture, thus protecting the animal from drying out. This quality frees a reptile from the need to live near water.

Most reptiles lay eggs with a leathery shell, within which the young develop fully to emerge similar in form to their parents. Unlike the amphibians they do not go through a larval stage after hatching.

Turtles have an upper and lower shell called, respectively, the carapace and the plastron. The carapace is attached to the backbone, for turtles are vertebrates.

All turtles have four limbs. The land tortoises have five toes on each foot, and the toes on the rear feet have no claws. The legs of the aquatic turtles have taken on the form of flippers, which makes swimming possible. Turtles have tails in addition to the four limbs.

Turtles have excellent vision because of their well-developed eyes which are equipped with three eyelids, one of which moves in from the side. The sense of hearing in these animals is poor, though they do have ears not visible above the skin. Their mouths lack teeth but are equipped with a horny rim which serves in their stead.

For the most part turtles are slow-moving animals, their main protection against their enemies being their ability to withdraw their bodies into the protection of the shell. Some turtles hibernate while others remain active throughout the year.

LOWER SIDE OF TURTLE
WITH LIMBS AND
HEAD EXTENDED

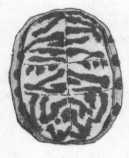

LIMBS AND HEAD
WITHDRAWN

WHERE TO FIND THEM

Turtles are usually found near a pond or a slow-moving stream. Certain species are very common in deserts, and others in eastern woodlands. Young turtles may be purchased for a trifling sum and the large, clumsy tortoise (another name for a land turtle) is sometimes found in gardens where people keep them as pets. If you buy a young turtle from a specialty shop, don't pick one that has been painted. This cruel procedure not only obscures the natural and beautiful markings on the carapace but inevitably results in the animal's death.

HOW TO KEEP THEM

The desert tortoise must have a large cage with a dry floor covered with sand or gravel. The baby turtles bought in shops should be kept in an uncovered container with straight sides that prevent the animal from climbing out. Inside the container there should be a bowl or sunken area filled with water. This miniature pool must be large enough for the turtle to swim in but not so deep or with such steep sides as to prevent it from climbing out onto the gravel. If a flat stone is placed as a bridge from the water to land it will make an excellent pathway for the small animal.

WHAT TO FEED THEM

The desert or box turtle eats mainly vegetable matter such as the outer leaves of lettuce, spinach, or any other edible greens. It will also relish cheese, hard-boiled or raw eggs, and fruit.

To feed the little turtles place them in a bowl of water. On the surface of the water scatter turtle food (bought at a variety or pet store). After the turtle has finished eating return it to the container. These little turtles will also eat bits of raw meat, earthworms, mealworms, cheese, and leafy vegetables in small quantities.

SAFETY NOTE: *Always have children wash their hands after handling baby turtles. A few cases of salmonella poisoning have developed in small children who have handled baby turtles and then put their hands in their mouths. There is no danger of this if hands are thoroughly washed.*

ACTIVITIES

1. Turtles are hardy and can stand a lot of handling. Because it is necessary to feed the little turtles in water they can be placed in the bowl by the children and when the animals are no longer interested in the food, they can be removed. After feeding the bowl should be emptied and washed before it is used again. The little turtles can be allowed to run about on the tables or floor, but keep a sharp eye on them for they are likely to disappear and not be found for several days. During this time they may have died from lack of water.

2. Watch the way the turtle tucks in its head, and how the neck seems to fold up.

3. Notice that the legs seem to close up the space between the shells and how in so doing they protect the head.

4. While the turtle's feet are still wet from feeding, place the animal on a piece of dark paper and notice the shape of its footprints. Does its tail also leave a mark?

5. Compare the turtle's feet, toes, and claws with our own hands.

6. Look into the turtle's mouth while it is feeding and notice its lack of teeth and the horny jaw with which it chews.

7. Look for the turtle's ears. (You won't find them for a turtle has no external ears.)

8. Observe the patterns of the marking on the shells, both carapace and plastron. They are sometimes quite beautiful and the children should be encouraged to copy them in their drawings. The separate divisions of the shells are called shields. These vary greatly in shape, those in the forepart being quite different from those near the tail, etc.

9. The children should be encouraged to draw and paint pictures of the turtles and to model them in clay.

10. Turtle dances could be invented. Shells of cardboard can be made and attached to the children so they can withdraw their arms, legs, and head between them.

11. Races between the baby turtles are sometimes fun for the children, but be careful lest the children step on them in their excitement.

12. If you are near a children's zoo, you will probably find that they keep some giant turtles from the Galapagos Islands. Viewing these friendly monsters is always worth the trip. In many zoos they are allowed to roam free among the children.

SOME HELPFUL MATERIALS

aquarium or bowl
rocks
turtle food
water

KEY VOCABULARY FOR CHILDREN

flippers
lower shell
*tortoise
upper shell

*Suggested for older children only

Bibliography

FOR ADULTS

Borror, Donald J. and DeLong, Dwight M. *An Introduction to the Study of Insects,* 3rd ed., New York, Holt, Rinehart & Winston, Inc., 1971.

Bronson, Wilfred S. *Turtles,* New York, Harcourt Brace Jovanovich, Inc., 1945.

Buchsbaum, Ralph *Animals Without Backbones,* revised 2nd ed., Chicago, University of Chicago Press, 1972.

Darling, Lois and Louis Darling *Turtles,* New York, William Morrow & Co., Inc., 1962.

Dethier, Vincent G. *To Know a Fly,* San Francisco, Holden-Day, Inc., 1963.

Earle, Olive *Crickets,* New York, William Morrow & Co., Inc., 1956.

Earle, Olive L. *Strange Lizards,* New York, William Morrow & Co., Inc., 1964.

George, Jean Craighead *All Upon a Stone,* New York, Thomas Y. Crowell Co., 1971.

Goudey, Alice E. *Red Legs,* New York, Charles Scribner's Sons, 1966.

Goudey, Alice E. *Here Come the Bees!* New York, Charles Scribner's Sons, 1960.

Hogner, Dorothy Childs *Snails,* New York, Thomas Y. Crowell Co., 1958.

Hawes, Judy *My Daddy Longlegs,* New York, Thomas Y. Crowell Co., 1972.

Hawes, Judy *What I Like About Toads,* New York, Thomas Y. Crowell Co., 1969.

Headstrom, Richard *Lizards as Pets,* Philadelphia, J.B. Lippincott Co., 1971.

Hegner, Robert W. *Parade of the Animal Kingdom,* New York, The Macmillan Co., 1967.

Hess, Lilo *The Remarkable Chameleon,* New York, Charles Scribner's Sons, 1968.

Life (periodical) *The Reptiles,* New York, Time-Life Books, 1963.

Life (periodical) *The Insects,* New York, Time-Life Books, 1962.

Lewis, H. L. *Butterflies of The World,* Chicago, Follett Publishing Co., 1973.

McClung, Robert M. *Ladybug,* New York, William Morrow & Co., Inc., 1966.

McClung, Robert *Moths and Butterflies and How They Live,* New York, William Morrow & Co., Inc., 1966.

Mitchell, Arthur A. *First Aid for Insects and Much More,* Irvington-on-Hudson, N.Y., Harvey House, Inc., 1964.

Mitchell, Robert T. and Zim, Herbert S. *Butterflies and Moths,* New York, Western Publishing Co., Inc., 1964.

Reid, George K. *Pond Life; A Guide to Common Plants and Animals of North American Ponds and Lakes,* New York, Western Publishing Co., Inc., 1967.

Silverstein, Alvin and Virginia Silverstein *Metamorphosis: The Magic Change,* New York, Atheneum Publishers, 1972.

Silverstein, Alvin & Virginia Silverstein *The Long Voyage; The Life-Cycle of a Green Turtle,* New York, Frederick Warne & Co., Inc., 1972.

Sterling, Dorothy *Insects and Homes They Build,* Garden City, N.Y., Doubleday & Co., Inc., 1954.

Urquhart, F. A. *Introducing the Insect,* New York, Frederick Warne & Co., Inc., 1966.

Villiard, Paul *Reptiles as Pets,* Garden City, N.Y., Doubleday & Co., Inc., 1969.

Zim, Herbert S. *Reptiles and Amphibians: A Guide to Familiar American Species,* New York, Western Publishing Co., Inc., 1956.

FOR CHILDREN

Carle, Eric *The Very Hungry Caterpillar,* New York, World Publishing Co., 1970.

Caudill, Rebecca *A Pocketful of Cricket,* New York, Holt, Rinehart & Winston, Inc., 1964.

Chenery, Janet *The Toad Hunt,* New York, Harper & Row Publishers, Inc., 1967.

Conklin, Gladys *I Like Butterflies,* New York, Holiday House, Inc., 1960.

Conklin, Gladys *We Like Bugs,* New York, Holiday House, Inc., 1962.

Conklin, Gladys *Lucky Ladybugs,* New York, Holiday House, Inc., 1968.

Conklin, Gladys *I Like Caterpillars,* New York, Holiday House, Inc., 1958.

Cromie, William J. *Steven and the Green Turtle,* New York, Harper & Row, Publishers Inc., 1970.

Darby, Gene *What Is a Butterfly?* Westchester, Ill., Benefic Press, 1958.

Darby, Gene *What Is a Frog?,* Westchester, Ill., Benefic Press, 1957.

Darby, Gene *What Is a Turtle?,* Westchester, Ill., Benefic Press, 1959.

Freschet, Berniece *Turtle Pond,* New York, Charles Scribner's Sons, 1971.

Huntington, Harriet E. *Let's Look at Reptiles.* Garden City, N.Y., Doubleday & Co., Inc., 1973.

Kellin, Sally M. *A Book of Snails,* Reading, Mass., Addison-Wesley Publishing Co., Inc., 1968.

Kepes, Juliet *Lady Bird Quickly,* Boston, Little, Brown & Co., 1964.

Mari, Iela *The Apple & The Moth,* New York, Pantheon Books Inc., 1969.

Marshall, James *Yummers!,* Boston, Houghton Mifflin Co., 1973.

Napjus, Alice and George Ford, *Freddie Found a Frog,* New York, Van Nostrand Reinhold Co., 1969.

Podendorf, Illa *The True Book of Insects,* Chicago, Children's Press, 1972.

Politi, Leo *The Butterflies Come,* New York, Charles Scribner's Sons, 1957.

Rockwell, Anne *Olly's Polliwogs,* Garden City, N.Y., Doubleday & Co., Inc., 1970.

Rood, Ronald N. *The How and Why Wonder Book of Ants and Bees,* New York, Grosset & Dunlap, Inc., 1962.

Russell, Franklin *The Honeybees,* New York, Alfred A. Knopf, 1967.

Selsam, Millicent E. *Let's Get Turtles,* New York, Harper & Row, Publishers Inc., 1965.

Selsam, Millicent E. *Terry and the Caterpillars,* New York, Harper & Row, Publishers Inc., 1962.

Stevens, Carla *Catch a Cricket,* Reading, Mass., Addison-Wesley Publishing Co., Inc., 1961.

3 Indoor Projects

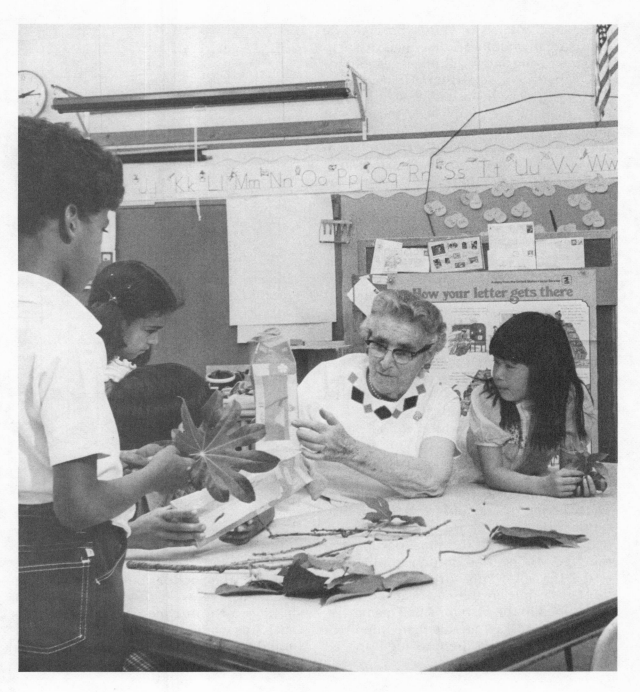

For small animals and birds that are to be kept for an indefinite time it is wise to provide strong and well-built cages, but for insects and other short-term tenants temporary cages can be fashioned at little or no cost. One of the simplest is the liter or quart-sized milk carton and an old nylon stocking or the stocking part cut from pantyhose. To make this cage cut a large window in one side of the carton and draw the stocking over the whole carton. This makes a cool, airy cage and is particularly appropriate for caterpillars. If a forked twig is set upright in the carton, the caterpillar will attach its cocoon or chrysalis to this instead of to the underside of the top where it can be observed only with difficulty.

Glass containers are somewhat dangerous for children to handle and they become too hot for the insects' well-being, as do plastic jars. Although many sorts of cages and containers can be purchased from pet stores, it is often more satisfactory for the children to make their own.

Water must be provided for all living organisms, whether plant or animal, though in some cases the food itself will furnish sufficient moisture. (The exceptions are noted in the specific projects.) Water containers should be such that they cannot be upset or do not present the danger of drowning the small occupant of the cage. An inverted bottle with the glass end of a medicine dropper inserted through a hole in the cork can be firmly suspended in the dish for small mammals.

Needless to say, an adequate supply of suitable food must be provided for all animals.

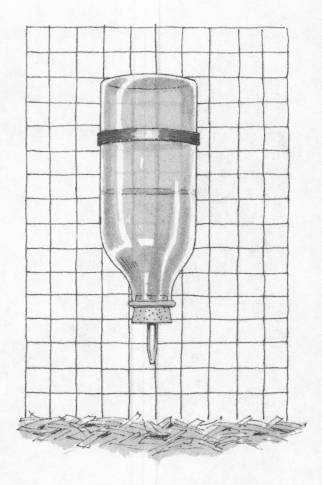

All containers must be kept clean; many of them should be cleaned daily, uneaten food removed, and fresh food and water supplied. The floor of a bird cage should be spread with gravel, and sawdust, wood shavings, or torn paper should carpet the cages of mammals. All these materials should be frequently cleared away and new provided.

Terrariums can be made in wide-mouthed, glass jars or in unused aquariums. The glass jars should have a screw top and the terrariums should be covered with a sheet of plastic or of glass which is fastened down tightly. Large mayonnaise jars, which can often be obtained from restaurants, should be laid in a horizontal position and firmly fixed in semicircular grooves cut into two small upright boards nailed to the baseboard. Long nails or screws may be substituted for the wooden end pieces, but are less attractive.

The bottom of a terrarium can be covered with moss, with the green side against the glass. On the moss put approximately 5 cm (2 inches) of gravel mixed with charcoal. (Bird gravel containing charcoal can be used for this purpose.) Well-rotted leaf mold and a centimeter (half inch) of forest soil should go above the gravel. After everything is in place the terrarium should be dampened with a light spray, and the inside of the glass wiped clean.

Now comes the planting: Use small plants dug from shady spots. Some may be found in the cracks of the pavement and between the curbstone and the sidewalk, or adhering to a stone or brick wall in the shade. Moss, tiny ferns, grasses, and other shade-loving plants will thrive in this tiny glass conservatory. If pieces of lichen or moss-covered rocks or driftwood are added to the arrangement, it will take on a more natural look. After everything is in place wipe the inside of the glass once more with a paper towel or rag before putting on the cover. If the terrarium is kept in a cool spot it will require only infrequent watering, for the cover prevents the water given off by the plants from evaporating. However, it may be wise to lift the cover for an hour or so when the inside of the glass "sweats". This will prevent the contents from mildewing. Small animals such as the slender salamanders or sowbugs live quite contentedly in such a terrarium and seem to find plenty of food for their needs.

For animals requiring a dry environment, terrariums should have dry sand or gravel on the floor and should be provided with a shallow dish for water.

SOME HELPFUL MATERIALS

aquarium containers
jars, large, wide mouth, with lids
milk cartons
nails or screws
saucers
stockings, nylon, or pantyhose
wood pieces

An
Aquarium

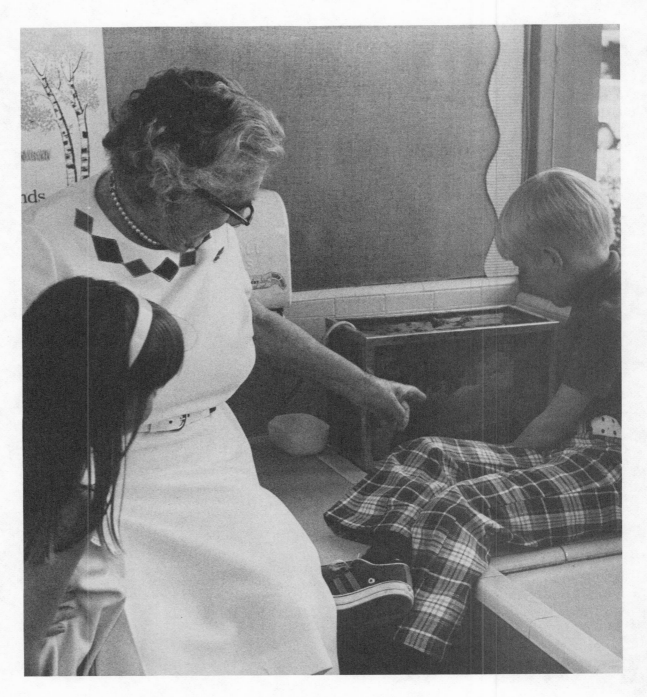

Children are often very interested in watching fish. In the classroom or at home an aquarium should be on display within eye range of the children, even at the expense of their putting their hands into the water.

HOW TO START A BALANCED AQUARIUM

A large glass bowl can be used, but better still, because of its straight sides which prevent distortion of view, is a rectangular aquarium with a capacity of not less than two gallons. The aquarium should be thoroughly cleaned before using by washing it with soap and water and rinsing it in running water three or four times. The bottom should then be covered to a depth of 5 cm (2 inches) with sand or gravel (if this is obtained from the beach it must be washed free of salt). Add water. Tap water should be allowed to stand for a couple of days before setting the plants in the gravel. Vallisneria, sagittaria, and ludwigia are some of the common aquatic plants that will root, while anacharis, cambomba, and myriophyllum are nonrooters that can also be grown. After placing the plants in the gravel, the aquarium can be filled to the top with water and placed in a spot where there is plenty of light but preferably not in direct sunlight, or the growth of algae will soon cloud the glass. After a few days stock the fish.

A heated tank is not necessary for guppies, though they will breed more rapidly at a temperature of about 24°C (75° F). Five or six fish, three males and two females, will reproduce in a short time and fill the aquarium to capacity. The fish require no care other than moderate feeding—a pinch of prepared food—every day. Feed only the amount that can be consumed in about five minutes. It will not harm the fish to remain unfed over the weekend, provided there are plants growing in the aquarium.

A six-gallon tank will support only three 5-cm (2-inch) goldfish, but double that number of fish half that size. A covered tank should be equipped with an air pump.

A few water snails will help to keep the glass clean, but the aquarium must be thoroughly washed from time to time. To do so remove the fish by means of a little dipper-net especially made for this purpose. The fish should then be transferred into water previously aged, the plants removed and washed, or replaced with new ones if needed. The gravel can be washed in running water. The tank is then replanted, filled with aged water, and the fish returned to it.

Guppies bear their young alive and the children will be interested in the tiny babies spawned from time to time. The female can be distinguished by the rounded body with a dark spot near the tail. This spot usually indicates the presence of young. As the body becomes more and more distended, indicating that the young are soon to be born, it is well to place the female in a specially designed strainer with coarse mesh. In this way the young will escape into the larger tank and their mother will be unable to eat them. The young can also escape by hiding among the growing plants or along the bottom of the aquarium in the gravel. As they grow larger the mother can be released from the strainer. At all times, the female is less lively than the male, which is more colorful and slender. It is interesting to watch the male trying to attract the interest of the female by swimming toward her, wriggling his handsome tail, then turning broadside before her in order to display his bright coloring.

Fishes have two pairs of fins, corresponding to the limbs of other animals, and one or two unpaired fins along the back and one on the belly. The tail is another fin and varies in shape on different species of fish. It is used primarily as a propeller, though in most fish the locomotion is achieved by a rhythmic contraction of the muscles, first on one side of the body, then on the other. This enables the fish to push against the water, first from one side and then from the other, weaving its way along. The paired fins maintain equilibrium and act as brakes.

A fish has no eyelids and thus sleeps with open eyes, remaining in one spot, its paired fins moving slowly all the while.

A fish breathes through its gills, covered by a flap which opens and closes each time the fish takes a breath. This is done by drinking in a mouthful of water, extracting the oxygen from it, and expelling it through the gills.

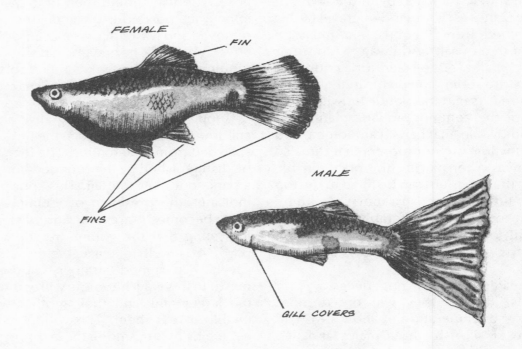

FEMALE
FIN
FINS
MALE
GILL COVERS

ACTIVITIES

1. The children might assist in selecting the fish at the pet shop.

2. They should feed the fish daily.

3. They could assist when the tank is cleaned by dipping out the fish and depositing them in the temporary container and later replacing them in the aquarium— but this is slippery work, so be on hand to help.

4. Pictures of the aquarium and of individual fish can be drawn, painted, or modeled from clay.

5. A fish dance can be composed, indicating the weaving motion through the water and the function of the fins.

6. If a hand is placed against the outside glass of the aquarium or above it, there is some reaction by the fish. Study this. It is unwise to allow the children to handle the fish even in the water because there is a covering of protective mucus, which if removed exposes the scales to infection.

7. In order to become better aquainted with the body of a fish one could be purchased from a fish market and brought in to be examined.

a. Observe the scales under a magnifying lens. They have growth rings similar to those on trees and the age of the fish can be estimated by counting the rings.

b. The gill covers can be operated by hand and the gills underneath examined.

c. The mouth should be opened and the roof and other parts examined.

d. The tail and fins should be spread and their form noted.

SOME HELPFUL MATERIALS

aquarium or fish bowl
aquarium plants
dipper net
fish from market
fish food
guppies (or other kind of fish)
sand
snails

KEY VOCABULARY FOR CHILDREN

fins
gills
gill covers
goldfish
guppies
scales
*tropical fish

*Suggested for older children only

A Cat
or a Kitten

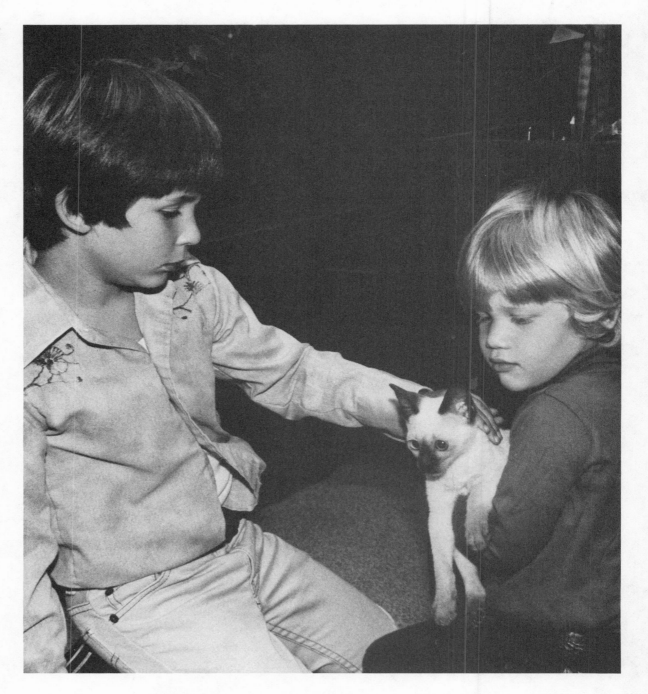

For this project borrow a cat or kitten that is accustomed to being around children so that it can be safely handled.

A cat is a mammal. Mammals are warm-blooded and have fur or hair and in most cases bear their young alive, nursing them from milk produced in the mammary glands. The cat is a carnivorous mammal with a muscular, lithe body, a rounded head, and pupils in vertical slits. The claws can be sheathed, or retracted, which protects them from becoming dull and enables the cat to creep up noiselessly on its prey. Cats have sharp, pointed teeth with long canines and they also have a keen sense of smell, hearing, and sight. They are able to see well in the dark because the retina reflects the smallest ray of light. That is why a cat's eyes seem to shine in the dark. Its whiskers too assist as feelers when there is little light to hunt by. The rough surface of the tongue is useful for licking and cleaning the fur and also for holding fast to the prey.

WHERE TO FIND ONE

Borrow a cat or a kitten, but it is best not to plan to keep it indefinitely, because the children will tire of it and because of the problem of caring for it during vacations and over weekends.

HOW TO KEEP IT

It is not likely that you will want to confine your cat or kitten in a cage, but if you do, remember that cats can jump, so the pen must be arranged with a lid so the animal can't get out. If the cat is kept indoors a litter box will be necessary for proper sanitation. This should be available to the cat or kitten at all times.

WHAT TO FEED IT

Give it cat food, fish, and milk. Cats also eat birds and mice, so keep your cat away from the bird feeder or the canary or mouse cage. See that a saucer of water is always available to the cat.

ACTIVITIES

1. The cat should be tame enough for the children to handle and cuddle. Encourage them to do so but do not allow them to dress it up in doll clothes or otherwise do unnatural things with it.
2. The children should feed the cat and keep its drinking saucer filled.
3. You can observe the cat's footprints by allowing it to walk over a very wet area and then onto dry paper. Or press a paw on an ink pad and then on paper. Notice that the claws do not show on the print because they are retracted. In this way they differ from the footprint of a dog.
4. Watch how the cat laps up water with its tongue. Have the children try to do this and they will be able to compare the surface of their own tongue with that of a cat.
5. Examine the large, upstanding ears with hairs that assist in catching sound.
6. Observe a cat's tail in order to follow its many moods: When angry it will lash its tail back and forth; when scared the tail seems to be much larger because the hairs stand straight out; when ashamed the tail will hang down.

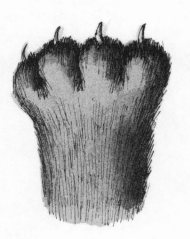

7. Listen to the many ways by which a cat "speaks". It will purr when relaxed, mew when you talk to it or to attract attention. It yowls when frightened and squalls when hurt. It has a special scream when it is fighting and everyone knows the sound a courting cat makes at night.

8. Cats like to be played with. A spool attached to a thread and pulled before a kitten will show the children how the animal pounces when it is hunting for mice.

9. Look into the cat's mouth and notice the rasps on the tongue used for holding prey and for combing its fur and observe the sharp pointed teeth, weapons of killing.

10. Observe and touch the whiskers, noticing how they extend beyond the width of the cat's body. This arrangement enables the cat, while crawling through narrow places, to acquaint itself with what surrounds it.

11. Watch a cat cleaning itself; see how it uses its tongue and its paws, how it cleans its face and the other parts of its body.

12. The children should be allowed to play with a kitten for the little animal likes to be tumbled about, chased and lifted, and so long as the children are not unduly rough the kitten will enjoy the play.

SOME HELPFUL MATERIALS

cat food
ink stamp pad
litter box
milk
saucers
spools
thread
water

KEY VOCABULARY FOR CHILDREN

claws
footprints
fur
mew
purr
whiskers

Dogs, like cats, are mammals. They are warm-blooded and have hair. Like most mammals they bear their young alive and have mammary glands for producing milk. Thus dogs can feed their young until they are ready for their carnivorous diet. Though dogs are meat eaters they will also eat other foods.

Dogs are related to such other canines as wolves, coyotes, and foxes. The wild members of the canine group have long, thin legs which enable them to run fast in order to catch their prey. They have long snouts and a very keen sense of smell, even keener than of vision. Dogs do not walk on the flat of the foot as we do, but on the tips of the toes. There are five toes on each foot, though one toe is much reduced in size. Their claws are blunt, useful for digging but not for clawing in fighting. As weapons the dog has a pair of sharp slashing teeth, the canines, in the front of the mouth. It also has molars in the back of the jaw for chewing.

The domestic dog has been hybridized for many years so that in many cases it no longer retains the same shape as the wild dog. For example, although the dachshund has a typical canine head, the short legs bred into the species enable it to hunt in holes for prey. Bulldogs were developed in England for baiting bulls. Their lengthened lower jaw and flat face give them a powerful grip.

WHERE TO FIND IT

A child-loving and gentle dog might be borrowed from someone. A very old dog does not want to be played with and while a puppy is lively and charming, a well-trained, house-broken dog certainly offers the least problems and is the most desirable for this project.

WHAT TO FEED IT

The owner of the dog should be asked whether to feed the dog while it is borrowed and if so what to give it. Water in a shallow dish should always be available for the dog to drink.

HOW TO CARE FOR IT

The dog should be borrowed only for a day at a time. If it is accustomed to being kept in the house, there should be no difficulty in tying it to some firm object by means of a fairly long leash so that it is not too closely confined.

ACTIVITIES

1. Encourage the children to pat it and otherwise handle and fondle it. If there are children who are afraid to do so they should not be forced or even urged to do so. But if they are to overcome their fear they should be invited to watch the other children playing with the dog. This may encourage the timid child to come nearer to the dog and eventually to pat it.

2. Feel the dog's nose and notice that it is covered with a soft, damp skin, slitted on the upper side. A dog's nose is very sensitive to the faintest odors. He uses it when approaching people to determine if they are friendly, to recognize other dogs and his human friends, to locate other dogs, and to warn him of the lurking enemy or of the prey he is hunting down.

3. Observe the dog's legs and compare them to those of the cat. The cat's bent legs enable it to stalk its prey and to spring, while the dog's are better for swift running, and are therefore in the typical dog long, thin, and straight.

4. Take the dog's footprints by allowing it to walk over a wet place and then onto a piece of dry paper or board. More permanent prints can be made by placing the dog's paw on an ink pad and then pressing it onto a sheet of paper.

5. Look outdoors for dog footprints in sandy or muddy spots and estimate the size of the dog that made them by comparing them to the footprints of the pet dog.

6. Compare a dog's footprint with that of a cat or a bird or with the child's own.

7. Notice how a dog pricks up his ears and turns his head when he wants to hear better. The upstanding ears catch sound waves.

8. While a dog's nose is his dominant sense organ, his eyes are better adapted to seeing in the dark than are our eyes. Like those of the cat they have a layer of retina that picks up the dimmest light and reflects it. That is why one can see a dog's eyes "shining" in the dark. Have the children observe this.

9. Observe the various ways dogs have of "talking." They whine when afraid, yelp when hurt, growl when angry, and bark when excited or ready to stand their ground against an enemy. The children might try to imitate these various sounds, guessing what they signify.

10. Watch the dog's tail. This also serves to tell us something of how he feels. The wagging tail means that the dog is friendly or happy; the stiff tail shows anger, and the tail between the legs that the dog is ashamed or sad.

11. A field trip to a pet shop or to the pound will enable the children to see many different breeds of dogs and to discuss dogs with the adults in charge.

12. If the children have dogs at home as pets, a dog-show might be arranged. This is best held outdoors and should not be competitive. Each dog should receive some sort of prize, as the smallest, largest, the brownest, the noisiest, etc.

SOME HELPFUL MATERIALS

dish
dog biscuits
ink stamp pad
leash
water

KEY VOCABULARY FOR CHILDREN

*canine teeth
 footprints
*molars
 odors
 prey

*Suggested for older children only

A Rabbit

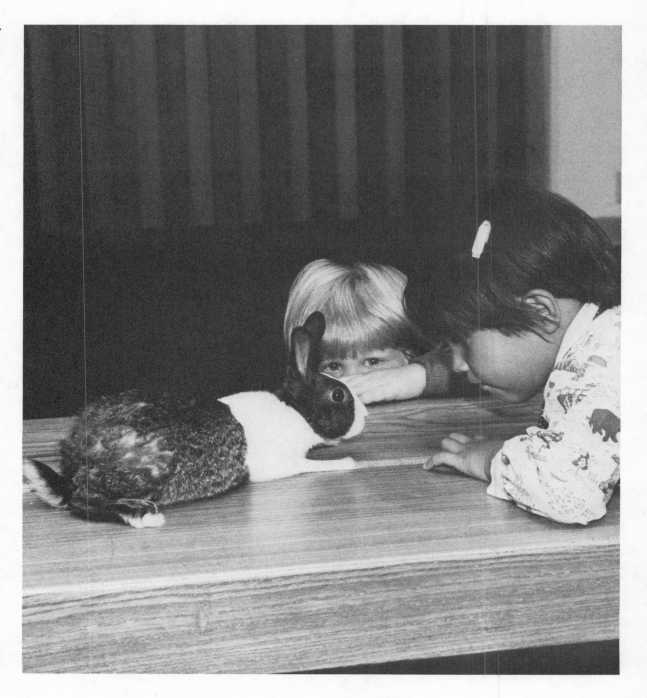

The rabbit is a mammal and is therefore warm-blooded, furry, and provided with mammary glands which produce milk for its live-born young. It is, however, not a rodent, or gnawer, though its front teeth continue to grow throughout the lifetime of the animal. Its cleft upper lip allows these cutting teeth full sway.

A rabbit's principal means of protection against its enemies is its long ears, which possess a keen sense of hearing. Unlike the hare, its close relative, it cannot run swiftly but can only hop because its hind legs are much longer than the front ones. The rabbit feeds mostly by night, and this nocturnal habit provides it with a certain amount of safety from large predatory birds and mammals that hunt by day. Rabbits also possess a good sense of smell and can often be observed wiggling their noses as they try to locate a scent at some distance. Their whiskers are tactile organs which help them to feel their way in the dark.

A rabbit will thump on the ground with its foot to warn others of its kind against approaching danger.

The female, or doe, is larger than the male rabbit. Both have short, very furry tails.

WHERE TO FIND IT

Though a wild rabbit might be trapped it is safer to buy one from a pet store. This will ensure that the pet is in good health and because it has been raised in captivity it is less likely to be afraid of being handled by the children. Rabbits can be safely cuddled in the arms but should not be lifted by the ears.

HOW TO CARE FOR IT

The rabbit should have a cage built of wire and wood with a 1 cm (½ inch) wire netting floor and a hinged top. The cage should be placed on a table or its own legs well above the drafty floor. Papers should be put beneath the cage to collect the droppings.

HOW TO FEED IT

The diet should be varied. Rabbit pellets, purchased from a pet store, should be a regular article of their diet; carrot, beet, and turnip tops, cabbage, sweet potato, and carrots are suitable foods. There should be a heavy dish with water in the cage and the water must be changed daily. Rabbits feed twice a day, morning and evening, the latter being the heavier meal. Keep the dishes used for the food scrupulously clean and remove any uneaten food from the cage every day. Sprinkle a little salt on the greens. DO NOT OVERFEED!

ACTIVITIES

1. The children should be allowed to cuddle the rabbit. This will be a good experience for them in learning how to handle a pet gently. If the rabbit is allowed out of the cage for any length of time place it on newspapers or you will have a job of cleaning up afterwards as a rabbit cannot be housebroken.

2. The children can help with the morning feeding and if there are afternoon classes the children attending can leave the evening's food. Do not encourage in-between treats.

3. The children can also help to clean the cage and the water dish, which they can fill with fresh water, and they might sprinkle the salt on the green food.

4. Make footprints of the rabbit and compare them with those of cats, dogs, or birds. To make these prints allow the rabbit to hop over a damp spot and then onto dry paper. You will notice that the prints of the small forefeet lie behind those on the hind feet.

5. More permanent footprints can be made by pressing the fore and hind foot on an ink pad and then on a piece of paper. This will show clearly the difference between the print of the forefeet and hindfeet.

6. Notice the shape of the droppings of the rabbit and compare with those of cats and dogs.

7. Observe the strong front teeth and the cleft upper lip. The sharp chisel-like edge of these teeth enables the rabbit to cut through grass and to gnaw, while the flat rear teeth are useful for chewing or grinding food to a pulp.

8. Notice how the rabbit can lift and turn its ears to catch sound.

9. Compare the texture of the whiskers with that of the fur on the body.

10. Count the toes on the forefeet and hindfeet.

11. Draw pictures and make clay models of the rabbit.

12. Compose a rabbit dance with the children imitating the rabbit hopping.

NOTE: A RABBIT SHOULD NOT BE MADE INTO A TOY AND THEREFORE SHOULD NOT BE DRESSED UP IN DOLLS' CLOTHES!

SOME HELPFUL MATERIALS

carrot, beet, turnip tops
ink pad
heavy dish
newspapers
plywood scraps
rabbit pellets
water
wire mesh, 1 cm (½ in.)

KEY VOCABULARY FOR CHILDREN

doe
female
furry
*mammal
thump
whiskers

*Suggested for older children

A live bird in the room may be a source of many interesting experiences. Though it is usually not advisable to hold it in one's hands, or to let it out of the cage, the children will enjoy watching the canary's actions.

The care of a canary must never be neglected and if the children tire of watching it bathe, or of helping to clean the cage and to fill the receptacles with seed and water, it is time to abandon this project and to turn the bird over to a more appreciative group of youngsters.

A canary is an herbivorous bird. Its thick, sharp-pointed bill is admirably adapted to cracking seeds and picking out the kernels. Its feet, with three toes in front and one behind, give it a firm grip on a perch, for this is one of the so-called perching birds. In sleep when the bird is relaxed the muscles of the leg tighten up in order to hold the bird firmly on the perch.

While the female canary is supposed only to chirp, it sometimes has quite an elaborate song. The male will sing during most of the year excepting during the weeks when it is shedding feathers, or molting. The feathers it sheds during this period will contribute to another project (see Feathers, pages 100–102).

A bird is warm-blooded with a temperature between 40-44°C (104° and 112°F). When excited its heart may beat as fast as 1000 times a minute and even under ordinary conditions a pigeon's heart beat is 192 and a sparrow's over 500 a minute. One can easily feel the heart beat when holding the bird in the hand and unfortunately as easily kill it by pressing over the spot where the heart is located.

HOW TO CARE FOR IT

A bird's cage must be kept clean. The paper covering its floor should be changed daily and fresh gravel spread on it. Water should be supplied daily and the water container thoroughly washed. The birdseed container must also be kept filled. A cuttlebone, which is generally enclosed in the box with the birdseed, should be inserted in the bars of the cage within reach of the bird's bill. The bill is kept sharp and clean by rubbing against the bone. Birds often relish the so-called tonics (available in pet shops), also fresh lettuce, celery, and a slice of apple which can be inserted between the bars of the cage and removed before they become moldy.

Some birds are tame enough to be released to fly about the room and to return to the cage if the door is left open. Don't experiment, however, unless you are sure your bird will go back to its cage, for it is difficult to catch a frightened bird. If the window happens to be open at the time it is released you may lose it altogether.

ACTIVITIES

1. Observe the bird carefully from time to time in order to learn about its body structures and how they are used: See how the tail is used to help the bird balance on its perch. (Unfortunately, how the tail is used in flight can't be observed if the bird can't be released from the cage. But the way a sparrow uses its tail can be observed outdoors and compared to the canary's actions in the cage.)

2. Notice how the wings are held close to the body and that they are composed of long, stiff feathers unlike the feathers that cover the body.

3. Observe the wings, composed of long flight feathers, three sets of coverts above and below, and the little tuft of feathers on the shoulder.

4. Notice that the breast feathers seem to stand out because of the padding provided by the contour feathers. Also notice the down beneath the breast feathers that insulates the bird against heat and cold.

5. Look at the legs and notice that they are covered with scales and that the toes have claws. In a captive bird these claws must be cut from time to time. A nail scissors can be used, but be sure to cut only the tips or the foot will bleed. The claws enable the bird to grasp the perch. Count the toes and note their position on the foot.

6. The children should assist in cleaning and caring for the bird. They should wash and fill the water and seed containers and insert them in the bars of the cage. They can also place the filled bath tub in the cage, and cut the paper to fit the floor of the cage.

7. Watch the bird bathing. Notice the sequence of splashing, ruffling the feathers, and preening. This the bird does by pulling the feathers through its bill, during which the bird may pause to sharpen the bill on the cuttlebone.

8. Compare the canary to other birds—the shape of the bill, the size and color of the body, and the songs it sings.

9. Notice how a bird keeps itself warm by fluffing out its feathers and thus making a blanket of air around its body. It does this when asleep too.

10. The children should have been allowed to visit the pet shop to pick out their bird. A later visit to the shop can be planned to talk to the dealer about canaries and their care and also to compare the color and other characteristics of their bird with some of those in the shop. At that time they will also in all probability see some other varieties of birds which will also be a source of discussion and comparison.

11. Notice the canary's sharp, black eyes and the way the bird will turn its head to watch the observer and to follow his or her actions.

12. A bird will often sing if there is noise or music audible. It will often "talk along" when the children are speaking. The only way to silence this is to cover the cage with a large cloth.

13. The children should try to mimic the bird's song, not just "peep-peep" but the actual rhythm, the rising and falling notes and their intervals.

14. If a bird is talked to, you can wait and expect a cheeping answer if the bird feels friendly and not alarmed.

15. If a female and male bird are placed in a large cage with nesting materials and a wire nest receptacle they may mate, lay eggs, and raise their young. If the young hatch, place a little dish with hard-boiled egg yoke softened with milk in the cage. The parents may feed the young this protein material.

16. The children can make drawings, paintings, and clay models of their bird.

SOME HELPFUL MATERIALS

apple
bird cage
birdseed
canary bath tub
canary nesting materials
celery
cuttlebone
dish
gravel
hardboiled egg
milk
newspapers

KEY VOCABULARY FOR CHILDREN

bill
claws
down
female
flight feathers
male
molting
preening
ruffling
scales

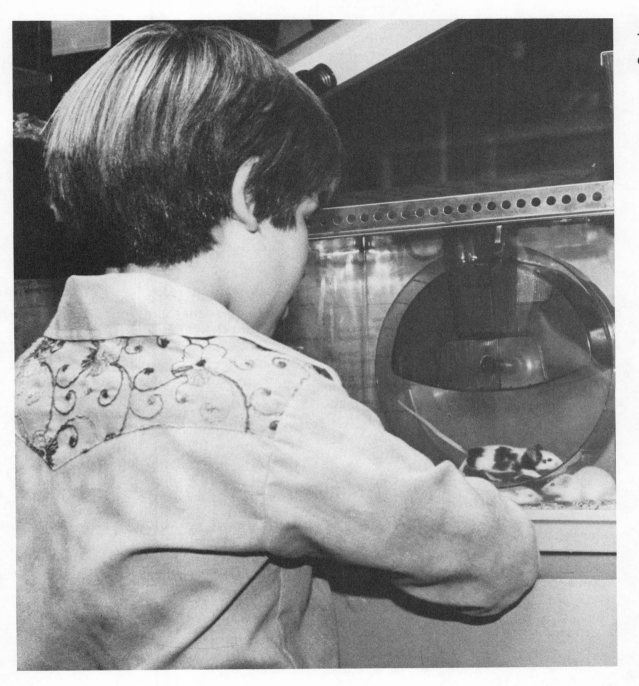

Mice are rodents characterized primarily by the continuous, lifelong growth of the front incisor teeth. Because these animals are gnawers their teeth get worn down on the outer surface and this continuing growth replaces what would otherwise be a useless stump. If a rodent has no chance to gnaw, these teeth will grow so long that the animal will be unable to close its mouth and will starve to death.

Rodents walk on the flat of the foot and they usually have five toes, although in some species the thumb is small or may be absent altogether.

There are a great many varieties of rodents besides mice and rats. These are squirrels, chipmunks, gophers, beavers, porcupines, and hamsters, to name only a few. And there are also many different sorts of mice.

The common house mouse has a tail that is apparently naked but if you look closely you will find that it is covered with fine hairs. This mouse is active not only by night, as are the field mice, but in the daytime as well. It cannot only climb but can also swim so it cannot be contained in a water-surrounded receptacle.

A house mouse makes its nest of any soft material, which it shreds for that purpose and the female will bear a litter five or more times a year regardless of season. The period of gestation is between 18 and 21 days and the number of young, which are born naked, varies from four to seven. It takes ten days before they are completely furred and fourteen days for their eyes to open. By the time they have reached the age of 35 days they are mature and can breed. Being a mammal, the mother mouse nurses her young, in her case for a little over three weeks.

WHERE TO FIND THEM

It is best to procure an albino mouse which has been bred in captivity, rather than a wild one you have trapped. This insures your having a healthy animal not carrying any disease germs. A mouse procured from a pet shop or from someone who breeds mice will be more apt to be tame and accustomed to being handled and is therefore less apt to bite.

HOW TO KEEP THEM

Mice should be provided with metal cages to prevent them from gnawing their way out. The floor should be removable and covered over with sawdust, wood shavings, or torn-up paper. Once a week this floor must be removed and thoroughly scrubbed and dried and fresh coverings placed on it. Food and water containers too should be removed and scrubbed with soap and water, thoroughly rinsed and dried. If the mice have made themselves rolls of bedding of the floor materials, replace these in the cage after it has been cleaned. A new, sectional, plastic caging is now available. This provides various tubes and passageways for the mice to explore, as well as excellent visibility.

WHAT TO FEED THEM

Water should be supplied from an inverted bottle suspended firmly at one side of the cage with easy reach of the mice. In

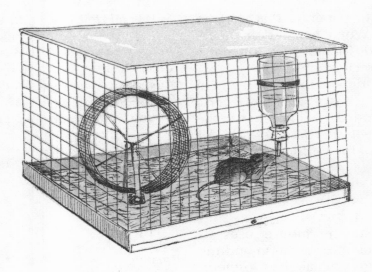

the neck of the bottle is a cork with a hole into which is inserted a tube. The glass end of a medicine dropper can be used for this purpose. The mice will drink by lapping off the drops that form.

Feed the mice bread crusts, grains, cereals such as uncooked rice, oats, cracked wheat or corn, sunflower seeds, peanuts, carrots, lettuce, food pellets, and from time to time bits of raw meat. Mice need not be fed daily provided there is enough food in the cage to last over the weekend or even longer. However, if insufficient food is left for the mother with young she will devour her own babies.

ACTIVITIES

1. If you are sure the mice can be safely handled, allow the children to nestle them in their cupped hands, but never to hold them by the tail or otherwise tease them. If mice are mishandled they learn to bite.

2. Place swings, ladders, and/or wheels inside the cage and watch the mice exercise. Such apparatus can be purchased at a pet store.

3. Breed the mice. There should be one male to two females and after breeding each female should be placed in a separate cage. The male may mistreat the female when they are first placed together. If so, he should be taken out and his cage placed close to hers for a couple of days. Then a second trial of placing them together should be made. After a few such separations they are likely to get along and mate.

After the young are born the male should again be removed for he is apt to eat his young.

After mating the female should be provided with shreds of wool, torn-up towels, wood shavings, or paper so that she can build her nest. When her abdomen becomes swollen do not disturb her more than necessary to clean the cage.

4. To make footprints of the mice let them run across a damp place and then over a dark, dry area. Notice the difference in the size of the forefeet and hindfeet and the relative position of the footprints when the mouse moves slowly and when it scurries.

5. Observe the shape and size of the droppings and compare to those of the hamsters, cats, and dogs.

6. Notice the way the mouse uses its whiskers as organs of orientation and the meticulous care the animal gives to them.

7. Compare the shape of the head to that of a dog, hamster, cat, or rabbit. Notice the use a mouse makes of its nose.

8. Look at the sharp, little eyes and compare with those of the other animals.

9. Gently feel the tail and compare the hairs on it to the fur on the mouse's body.

10. Allow the children to assist with the feeding, filling of the water bottle, and cleaning of the cage.

11. Make drawings of the mice or paintings and models in clay.

12. The children might compose a mouse dance, crouching, running, scurrying, etc.

SOME HELPFUL MATERIALS

bottle with cork and glass tube
cage, metal
food, wide variety–grains, etc.
mouse toys
wood shavings or torn up paper

KEY VOCABULARY FOR CHILDREN

gnaw
gnawers
*incisor teeth
*litter
*mating
*nursing
*rodents

*Suggested for older children only

Like mice hamsters are rodents, a group of animals with incisors, or front teeth, that continue to grow as long as the animal lives. Because rodents are gnawers, this continuous growth serves the purpose of replacing the cutting edge of the teeth as it is worn away. The outer surface of the teeth is of a harder material than the inner and thus wears away more slowly, so that the incisors are self-sharpening chisels. If the teeth are not used daily for gnawing on hard food and other objects, the upper ones will grow too long and turn inward and upward and may in time pierce the roof of the mouth. Unlike mice hamsters have little body odor and have relatively few diseases. For this reason they make good pets for the classroom.

Most rodents have five toes on each foot (the thumb in some of these animals may be absent) and all rodents walk on the flat of the foot. The tail is easily broken off, which allows the animal to leave it in the mouth of an enemy while escaping. Later the tail will grow again. On hamsters the tail is extremely short. They stuff the food they gather into their cheek pouches, which when filled protrude on both sides of the head like swellings. In the wild the hamster will empty the contents of the cheek pouches into a burrow dug in the ground in fields or open meadows.

Hamsters have from six to fifteen young in a litter, fewer during the winter months, and the babies may be born during any month of the year. They are naked and blind at birth but before they are two weeks old are fully grown and capable of breeding.

WHERE TO FIND THEM

Hamsters are not native to the North American continent. They were brought here from Syria in 1938. They must be obtained from a pet shop or from someone who breeds them. Sometimes the laboratories in hospitals will give them away.

HOW TO CARE FOR THEM

Because the hamster can gnaw through wood a metal cage must be provided where the bottom is covered with .5cm-1cm (¼ inch-½ inch) wire mesh. On this place wood shavings, excelsior, or paper torn into strips, to furnish the hamster with material to build its burrow. Even if the bottom of the cage is not of wire mesh, sawdust or wood shavings must be supplied. Hamsters should be kept in a warm place or they will hibernate. A new plastic tunnel-caging is also available in some pet shops.

WHAT TO FEED THEM

An inverted bottle with a tube protruding through the cork should be suspended against one side of the cage. This is kept filled with water. The hamster will lick off the drop that hangs there and get enough water for its needs.

Dog biscuits, rabbit pellets, or poultry feed and grain must be provided as the hamsters must have hard food to chew on. In addition to this they should be fed green vegetables, such as cabbage, lettuce, celery tops, and bits of fruit, apples or apple parings, grapes, and even a bit of meat from time to time. Do not overfeed—every other day is enough.

ACTIVITIES

1. These are tame little animals and can be handled. The children will enjoy fondling them. However, before the animals become accustomed to the children they may be frightened and if so will bite. SO GO SLOWLY! A hamster should be picked up by the loose skin at the back of its neck.

2. Compare your hamster with mice and rats or with a kitten, dog, or rabbit. Notice its short tail, its longish, golden-brown fur, its large, pointed ears and its big, dark eyes.

3. Examine its forefeet and hindfeet and notice that the former have only four toes while the latter have five, all of which are tipped with claws. Have the children discuss the purpose of these claws.

4. The children can assist in cleaning the cage, providing fresh water and food. The cleaning need not be done more often than once a week provided that it is thoroughly carried out. The water bottle should be washed at the same time, and the tube cleaned by allowing water to run through it. Food and water should be supplied and any not eaten thrown out. It is safe to leave hamsters for as long as four days if they have been supplied with pellet food and a full water bottle.

5. Make footprints of the hamsters by letting them run through a damp place and then over dry paper, or by pressing the feet, one at a time, onto an ink pad then onto paper.

6. Have the children make clay models of the hamsters and draw and paint pictures of them.

7. Watch the hamsters eating and observe how the cheek pouches swell out. Then observe what the animals do with the contents of the pouches. It is possible that you may find it difficult to observe this as the hamsters prefer to feed at night.

8. Imitate the locomotion of the hamsters and compare this with the way a rabbit gets around. You will notice that, unlike the rabbit, the hamster does not have the long rear legs that would enable it to hop.

9. Hamsters can be successfully bred in captivity. For instructions see the books listed in the Bibliography (page 84).

SOME HELPFUL MATERIALS

bottle with cork and tube
cage, metal
dog biscuits
grain products
rabbit pellets
wood shavings or paper strips

KEY VOCABULARY FOR CHILDREN

burrow
cheek pouches
claws
*forefeet
fur
gnaw
gnawers
*hindfeet
*incisors

*Suggested for older children only

Bibliography

FOR ADULTS

Bethell, Jean *How to Care for your Dog*, New York Four Winds Press, 1969.

Bond, Gladys B. *Album of Cats*, Chicago, Rand-McNally & Co., 1971.

Bronson, Wilfred *Dogs, Best Breeds for Young People*, New York, Harcourt, 1969.

Buck, Margaret Waring *Small Pets from Woods and Fields*, Nashville, Tenn., Abdingon Press, 1960. pages 10-11 (terrariums), page 21 (amphibians), pages 30-31 (lizards and turtles), pages 41, 45, 47 (insects and spiders), pages 58-60 (mammals), pages 66-67 (birds), pages 42-43 (vivariums)

Case, Marshal T. *Look What I Found! The Young Conservationist's Guide to the Care and Feeding of Small Wildlife*, Riverside, Conn., Chatham Press, 1971. pages 11-16 (terrariums, aquariums, collecting equipment), pages 23-24 (caterpillars), pages 25-28 (ants), pages 39-42 (frogs and toads), pages 43-45 (salamanders), pages 48-51 (turtles), pages 54-55 (lizards), pages 57-59 (mice), page 61 (rabbits), page 86 (hamsters)

Chrystie, Frances N. *Pets*, Boston, Little, Brown & Co., 1964. pages 56-57 (mice), pages 59-60 (hamsters), pages 65-66 (canaries)

Gilbert, Mirium *Science-Hobby Book of Aquariums*, Minneapolis, Minn., Lerner Publications Co., 1970.

Greenberg, Frances S. and Edith L. Raskin *Home-Made Zoo*, New York, David McKay Co., Inc., 1952. pages 3-6 (hamsters), pages 92-96 (birds)

Jacobson, Ethel *The Cats of Sea-Cliff Castle*, Los Angeles, Ward Ritchie Press, 1972.

Metcalf, Christine *Cats: History, Care, Breeds*, New York, Grosset & Dunlap, Inc., 1970.

Paysan, Klaus *Aquarium Fish from Around the World*, Minneapolis, Minn., Lerner Publications Co., 1970.

Pettit, Ted S. *A Guide to Nature Projects*, New York, W. W. Norton & Co., Inc., 1966. pages 49-51 (flies), pages 129-133 (terrariums), page 163 (crickets), pages 164-167 (ants), pages 174-179 (frogs and toads), pages 179-180 (salamanders), pages 183-184 (turtles), pages 184-185 (lizards), page 286 (chipmunks), page 287 (mice)

Pringle, Laurence, ed. *Discovering Nature Indoors: A Nature and Science Guide to Investigations with Small Animals*, Garden City, N.Y., Natural History Press, 1970. pages 7-28, 32-48 (terrariums and aquariums), pages 29-31 (turtles), pages 68-77 (houseflies), pages 82-84 (ants), pages 86-94 (earthworms), pages 105-119 (mice)

Ricciuti, Edward R. *Shelf Pets; How to Take Care of Small Wild Animals*, New York, Harper & Row, Publishers Inc., 1971. pages 3-12 (housing and feeding), pages 13-27 (frogs and toads), pages 28-36 (salamanders), pages 54-65 (lizards), pages 66-74 (turtles), pages 75-79 (spiders), pages 88-91 (caterpillars), pages 92-97 (grasshoppers), pages 98-100 (millipedes), pages 108-115 (snails), pages 116-120 (hamsters)

Silverstein, Alvin and Virginia Silverstein *Rabbits: All About Them*, New York, Lothrop, Lee & Shepard Co., 1973.

Villiard, Paul *Exotic Fish as Pets,* New York, Doubleday & Co., Inc., 1971.

Wong, Herbert H. and Matthew F. Vessel *Our Terrariums,* Reading, Mass., Addison-Wesley Publishing Co., Inc., 1969.

FOR CHILDREN

Blegvad, Lenore and Erik Blegvad, *The Great Hamster Hunt,* New York, Harcourt Brace Jovanovich, Inc., 1969.

Finley, Virginia and Beverly Mason *A Cat Called Room 8* New York, G. P. Putnam's Sons, 1966.

Fisher, Aileen *Listen Rabbit,* New York, Thomas Y. Crowell Co., 1964.

Hess, Lilo *Rabbits in the Meadow,* New York, Thomas Y. Crowell Co., 1963.

Lionni, Leo *Fish Is Fish,* New York, Pantheon Books, Inc., 1970.

McClung, Robert M. *Whitefoot, The Story of a Wood Mouse,* New York, William Morrow & Co., Inc., 1961.

Selsam, Millicent *How Puppies Grow,* New York, Four Winds Press, 1971.

Simon, Seymour *Discovering What Goldfish Do,* New York, McGraw-Hill Book Co., 1970.

Stoutenburg, Adrien *A Cat Is,* New York, Franklin Watts Inc., 1971.

Wildsmith, Brian *Brian Wildsmith's Fishes,* New York, Franklin Watts, Inc., 1968.

4   *Watching Things*

Hatching Chickens

You might procure for this interesting project a brooding hen and a clutch of fertile eggs, but having a setting hen is not always the wisest procedure. The hen can sometimes be the cause of tragedy when one of the chicks in this confined area is inadvertently injured and is then victimized by the hen and other chicks, which may peck it to death. For this reason an incubator might be preferable and can be constructed or bought and stocked with fertile eggs—not those purchased at a grocery store but from a poultry farm that specializes in fertile eggs. An inexpensive incubator stocked with quail eggs which can be purchased at low cost is also available by writing to Natural Science Industries, 15-17 Rockaway Beach Blvd., Far Rockaway, N.Y. 11691. The baby quails make excellent pets.

An incubator can be made with a carton having one side of glass, so the children can look in. This is especially desirable while the chicks are hatching out. The container must be kept at a constant temperature between 39°—41°C (102°—106°F). Place an electric bulb and a thermometer inside the incubator to check the temperature. A 60-watt bulb should keep the temperature within this range. The bulb should be turned off when the temperature gets too high, and on when low temperature is reached. A thermostat in the circuit is helpful. The eggs must be turned once or twice a day so that they will be evenly warmed and air will reach their interior. Chicken eggs are tapered to a narrow end and thus fit together in a cluster in the nest and are covered by the body of the setting hen.

A dish of water should be left in the incubator at all times to produce the necessary humidity. The shell of an egg is porous, admitting oxygen and allowing waste gases to escape, as evidenced by the fact that an egg put under water will admit water and drown the embryo inside. In addition to the white and yolk, eggs contain a tiny, life-bearing, jellylike cell that lies on the yolk. The yolk and the white, protein, supply food for the unhatched chick. The white also serves to cushion it from shock. An air sac at the large end of the egg contains enough air to supply the chick during the long and arduous period of hatching. At this time the tiny bird possesses a tool—a horny egg tooth at the tip of the upper bill—with which it first cracks the shell, then pries it open. The eggs hatch in 21 days after conception. It is important to find out how many days have passed when you get the eggs, so you can be ready when the chicks break through. Even though getting out of the egg is a very difficult process for the chicks, you must never help them. They need this exercise for greater strength later on.

HOW TO CARE FOR THE CHICKS

Once hatched the birds must be fed and should be given a place to run about in and a warm spot for cuddling during the night. Though canaries and many perching birds are born naked, helpless, and quite ugly until their feathers grow, chickens and ducks have a soft nestling down and strong legs so that they are able to run about and pick up their own food only a short time after hatching.

WHAT TO FEED THEM

Food should be purchased from a poultry supply house and water must be provided.

ACTIVITIES

1. Watch and record by children's drawings or by photographs taken by the teacher the sequence of events starting with the building of the incubator, the purchasing of the eggs, and the visit to the poultry farm. Record the placing of the eggs in the incubator, the hatching and emergence of the chicks. These pictures will make a fine scrapbook for the children.

2. The chicks can be held by the children and will nestle in the cup of the hand.

3. The children can assist with the feeding and cleaning of the enclosure in which the chicks are kept.

4. The presence of the chicks might suggest dances, pageants, etc.

SOME HELPFUL MATERIALS

cage for chicks
dishes
eggs, fertile
food for chicks
incubator, commercial or made from box, glass
panel, electric light, thermostat (optional)
thermometer
water

KEY VOCABULARY FOR CHILDREN

chick
down
*fertile egg
hatching
incubator
thermometer

*Suggested for older children only

A Feeding Tray for Birds

While not all school rooms face a lawn or garden—locations that attract birds—a feeding tray placed outside the window will in many cases bring birds for observation, if only pigeons, starlings, and English sparrows. Such a tray can be either put on a pedestal or fastened to a shelf outside the window. In either situation the tray must be protected from cats by means of a railing made of jagged points of tin or of barbed wire.

More than bread must be provided for food as birds have different feeding habits and foods of many sorts are needed to attract a variety of birds.

The feeding tray should be placed far enough away from the observers that the birds will not be frightened away, and not so far away that the children can't distinguish details, such as coloring and other markings, bills and feet.

During different seasons of the year the species of birds will change. In other words migrants will stop to eat as they go to and from their nesting areas. Summer and winter visitors stay for the whole season and resident birds stay in the vicinity throughout the year.

It will be interesting to observe how the large and small birds get along together; which birds come alone and which in flocks; which eat which sort of foods; the way each species of bird eats; how the birds approach the feeding table (from the ground, direct from the air, or by flying in from a nearby shrub or tree from which they have been watching the table cautiously for a while.) Some birds dominate others, even within a flock. One bird will always feed before the others, which will not move in until the dominant one has finished eating. There are pugnacious birds and meek ones, there are clever ones which can figure out the solution to a difficult situation, and there are those that are easily discouraged and fly away after one attempt to solve their problem.

The adaptations of bodily form for feeding should be observed—the thick bills of seed-eating birds, the slender bills of insect and other protein seekers, the long, thin bills of hummingbirds, suitable for dipping deep into flowers for nectar and the insects floating in it. There are also the general utility bills of such birds as robins, indicating a diet that includes berries and worms.

Birds have other adaptations too, such as long narrow wings for sustained flight over long distances, long legs for feeding in marshy places, and webbed feet for wading and swimming, but these are not so easily observed at a feeding table.

Watch for birds that leave the feeding table with food in their mouths. They might be taking back food for their young.

WHAT TO FEED THE BIRDS

The birds can be fed wild birdseed or suet. The suet can either be nailed down to the feeding tray or hung nearby on a string, or put in a container made of coarse meshed wire nailed against an upright in such a way that it can be opened for replenishment. Suet can often be obtained free from a butcher. Peanut butter mixed with bird seed and inserted between the bracts of a pine cone can be hung above or

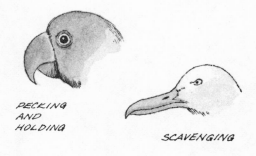

BEAK ADAPTATIONS

PECKING AND HOLDING

SCAVENGING

PROBING

TEARING AND KILLING

SEED EATING

BOTTOM FEEDING

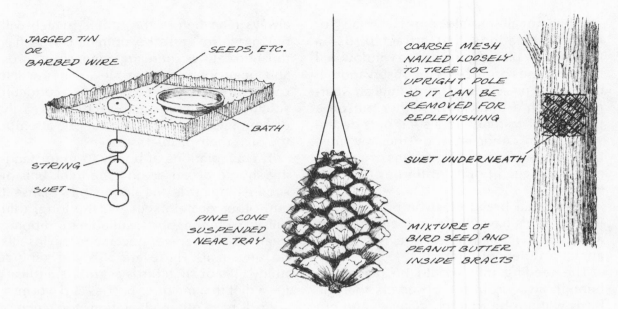

JAGGED TIN OR BARBED WIRE

SEEDS, ETC.

BATH

STRING

SUET

PINE CONE SUSPENDED NEAR TRAY

MIXTURE OF BIRD SEED AND PEANUT BUTTER INSIDE BRACTS

COARSE MESH NAILED LOOSELY TO TREE OR UPRIGHT POLE SO IT CAN BE REMOVED FOR REPLENISHING

SUET UNDERNEATH

near the feeding tray. Some birds will peck at nut meats, the inside skin of melons, or sunflower, pumpkin, and squash seeds, and fruits of all kinds. By placing a large, shallow basin filled with water on the tray the birds will not only drink but may bathe too. The large terracotta saucers used under flower pots are suitable for this purpose because of their size and weight, which prevent their being tipped over. The water must be frequently changed.

ACTIVITIES

1. Because the tray is always visible the children can watch it from time to time and should be encouraged to make their own observations. They can be assisted by the teacher's calling attention to characteristics of different species, such as special markings like stripes on the head or wing bars, speckled or streaked breasts, the shape of the bill, the color of the tail, back or underparts, and many other details. A diagram of a bird showing the different parts of the body would assist the children when they want to describe what they have seen.

2. The children should help to place the food on the tray and to bring some of the items mentioned above from home for this purpose. They can also see that the basin is kept filled with clean water. This can be done with a long-spouted watering can.

3. The children can play at being birds at the feeding table, at flying away when alarmed, pecking at one another or peacefully at the food. This dramatic play could be turned into a dance.

4. They can make drawings, paintings, and models of the different birds and have an exhibit for parents or other children, centered around the bird feeding table as subject matter.

5. The bird songs and twitterings can be mimicked. These should not be merely "cheep-cheeps" but the rhythms and rising and falling notes should be noted and copied. A game might be made of this as to which bird a child is impersonating both by its actions and by its song.

6. The children's observations need not be confined to the birds visiting the feeding tray for spilled food attracts different birds. In addition there are birds that do not come to the feeding tray at all. These can be compared with those that do. A squirrel may get wind of the free food and come to feed too, but this will not harm the birds, as a stray cat surely would. (NOTE: Do not encourage the children to call cats "bad". They are predatory animals and birds are a regular item of a cat's diet.)

7. An outdoor bird bath in the vicinity of the feeding tray will also provide some interesting observations of bird life.

SOME HELPFUL MATERIALS

basin, large
bird bath
birdseed
hammers
nails
peanut butter
pine cones
water
wire, meshed, coarse
wood

KEY VOCABULARY FOR CHILDREN

berries
bills
bird feeder
birds' songs
breasts
feathers
seed
suet
tail
worms

A Wasps' Nest

Wasps are insects, with all the characteristics of this group of animals (see Bees, pages 25–27). They can be distinguished from bees by the narrow waist, where the thorax joins the abdomen. Like bees their sting is situated at the tip of the rear end of the abdomen. Unlike bees they eat not only pollen and nectar but animal food, meats, and sweets from our table as any picnicker will attest.

In the autumn when the paper-making wasps desert their large, grey nests, an empty nest may be found and brought into the room. The nest is made of wood pulp or foliage combined with the wasps' saliva. This chewed-up material is tamped onto the outside of the nest in tiny bits, usually in rows, which are often of different colors.

Because wasps' nests are occupied for only one season, they are deserted in the fall when all but the queen wasp dies. The larvae still in the hexagonal cells die of neglect and can be pried out and examined in order to follow the various stages of development from pupa to adult. There is no store of honey in these nests because paper wasps bring their young only bits of meat, such as the bodies of insects they have stung to death, and also portions of the flesh of larger animals.

The diet of the adults has a wider range as it may include nectar from flowers, ripe fruit and sticky, sweet substance produced by other insects. Some of this food is also fed to the larvae. In exchange the adults receive a sweet fluid.

Some paper wasps build open nests with the larva cells exposed. Others (largely hornets) build closed, or protected nests.

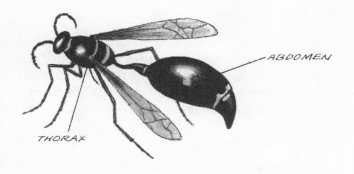

Hornets' nests, like wasps' nests, are protected by an outer covering of "paper." They vary in size: there are small, unfinished ones built in the early spring by the queen but often abandoned. Some of these are shaped like inverted cups and others are almost spherical. All of these small nests have only a few cells, in some of which eggs have been laid. The larger hornets' nests have been developed from such small ones and in enlarging them the outer walls are taken down and new ones built. The cells are constructed in tiers, each attached to the one above. Sometimes a large nest will consist of many stories.

WHERE TO FIND A WASPS' NEST

Sometimes wasps' nests can be found on the ground, where they have been knocked down, and sometimes they can be found attached to the undersurface of overhanging roofs or other protected spots. If you plan to take one of these down, watch it beforehand for a while to be sure that no wasps are still using the hole—that it is truly abandoned.

HOW TO KEEP THE NESTS

These nests require no care, but like all objects on exhibition they should not be kept for too long, for once the children have seen and handled a nest, it becomes only a dust collector.

ACTIVITIES

1. Break off bits of the paper and compare it by touch to man-made paper. Try writing on it with pencils or crayons.

2. Make some paper by mixing sawdust and a bit of water, or by mashing up shreds of paper in water, and then laying it out in thin sheets to dry.

3. Explore the cells in the nest and pry out any pupae remaining in them. These may be in any stage of development and should be compared one with another.

4. Examine the construction of the tiers inside the nest and look for the paper supports by which each is suspended from the one above.

5. Trap some wasps or yellow jackets by placing food, especially sweets or meat, outside and popping a glass over them.

6. These insects have a painful though usually not dangerous sting and should not be handled, but they may be observed moving inside the glass. Note their six legs, antennae, and three-sectioned bodies, their compound eyes, and the mouthparts. Notice also the two pairs of papery wings folded along the sides of the body when not in use.

7. The children can draw pictures of the nest showing both the outside shape and the six-sided cells inside.

SOME HELPFUL MATERIALS

paper wasps' (hornets') nest
pencils
sawdust
tumbler, clear glass
water

KEY VOCABULARY FOR CHILDREN

cells
hornets
larva
paper wasps
queen

Birds build their nests in various ways, each species of bird using material and methods that differ from all the others. Some birds build on the ground, others in holes, and still others in trees, bushes, the eaves of houses, and many other spots. In some instances the nest is built by the female, in others by the male and in still others by both birds in cooperation. Some nests are very elaborate and others are merely shallow depressions in the ground, in the sand, or among pebbles or leaves that serve to conceal them. There are even parasitic birds that build no nests at all, laying their eggs in the nests of other birds.

Some nests are constructed of mud, like those of some swallows, and adhere to the walls of buildings because the mud is mixed with the birds' own saliva. Robins also use mud but only to strengthen and line their nests, which are made of grass and twigs for the most part. Soft, cottony materials, such as thistledown, are used by certain birds and hummingbirds build their nests of lichen and spider web silk. Nests are frequently lined with soft feathers the mother bird plucks from her own breast.

The location selected for nest building is usually not far from where the necessary materials are found, in the vicinity perhaps of a pond where mud of the correct consistency can be procured or where grass or twigs are abundant.

Nests are necessarily constructed with bills and feet and in some cases the ingenuity and skill displayed is truly astounding. The bird uses its own body to shape the nest to the right-sized cup appropriate for its eggs and young.

WHERE TO FIND THEM

Never take a nest still in use! To locate such a nest watch the comings and goings of birds from a certain location, for this may indicate either that a nest is being built or that the nestlings are being fed. Observe what the birds are carrying in their beaks and if the burden is an insect you will know that the nestlings are hatched and are being fed. A nest is not occupied for more than the time it takes to raise the young, in most cases not more than a few weeks. As soon as the fledglings can fly the nest is deserted. However, some birds return to the nest they built in previous years.

WHAT TO DO WITH AN ABANDONED NEST

1. A nest still in place on a tree should be examined to determine the way it was fastened to the supporting object, such as a branch. A nest must be secure in order to prevent the eggs or nestlings from falling out.
2. Notice the white excrement around the edges of the nest. This will indicate how birds keep the cup of the nest clean and prevent their nestlings from fouling themselves.
3. If you plan to bring in the abandoned nest for observation, leave it for a few days

outside on a piece of paper in case it is infested with mites. If so it is better not to handle it or to bring it in because the mites will move over onto human subjects. If the nest is an old one that has wintered over it is quite safe to have the children handle it. Now look it over carefully to observe the materials of which it was built—grass, twigs, mud, etc. Notice too the man-made objects incorporated in the structure. Some birds are quite fond of decorating their nests with shiny or white objects.

4. After more or less tearing the nest apart gather up the scraps and plant them in a flowerpot with soil above and below. Then water the pot and in a few days you may find that a number of different plants will sprout from the seeds in the building materials. (If you want to be sure that the seeds were not in the soil, you can sterilize it with boiling water or by baking it for a while in the oven before using it for planting the nest.)

5. Search the ground under or near an abandoned nest for bits of eggshells. (Unfortunately you may also find a dead nestling that has fallen from the nest.) Compare the egg shell scraps with a hen's egg, or a robin's blue egg shell with the brown and purplish spotted egg shell of the house sparrow. Note the difference in size, indicating the size of the hatching bird.

ACTIVITIES CONNECTED WITH AN OC-CUPIED NEST

1. Watch the parent bird bring back food and remove the excrement from the nest.

2. Sit down and watch the birds coming and going, and after the parent birds have left take a look inside the nest. If there are still eggs there do not remove them or even touch them, but observe their color, number, size, and their neat arrangement in the nest, with the small end of the egg to the center of the nest.

3. Time the comings and goings (for older children) and notice how many times they come back within a half hour.

4. If the young are being brooded or fed, observe how the parent birds return to the nest, making every effort to conceal its location by seldom approaching it in a direct line; how they will often wait on a neighboring branch with food in the bill and look around for a while before making a dart to the nest.

5. If the children are able to see into the nest without being observed themselves by the parent birds, have them notice that the nestling stretching its head up the highest and making the most commotion is the first to be fed. The bright interior of the tiny birds' mouths, surrounded by the gayly colored open beaks, attracts the attention of the parent so that the food is dropped into the most prominent opening. One would suppose that the hungriest nestling would call loudest for food, but this is not always the case.

6. During the nesting season it is sometimes possible to entice birds to build nearby either by furnishing bird houses or by hanging nesting materials in a prominent place. Use string not more than two inches in length, excelsior, straw, cotton, or twigs.

SOME HELPFUL MATERIALS

birds' nests
flowerpots or paper cups
garden soil
magnifying glasses
newspapers
tweezers
water

KEY VOCABULARY FOR CHILDREN

feathers
grass
mud
seeds
spider web silk
twigs

Looking
at Feathers

There are a number of differently shaped feathers on a bird's body. There are the various types of contour feathers and down. Contour feathers are of two sorts, those with curved shafts that follow the contour of the body, and the wing and tail feathers, used in flight. The latter have a stiff shaft with a bare, hollow part known as the quill and a grooved, tapering portion supporting the barbs. The quill and the barbs, with their intricate hooking devices, form the vane. The barbs are not only attached to the shaft but also to the barb ahead and behind by means of tiny hooks, called barbules. These in turn are attached to one another by even smaller hooks. This is what gives the finely interwoven surface to the vane and makes it strong enough to support a bird in flight.

Not all contour feathers have such hooks. Some have short, curved shafts and as they hug the bird they act as a covering that entraps air, much as a feather bed does for us by insulating the body from heat and cold.

Down feathers lack a shaft altogether. Newly hatched birds are covered with down only. It is also present beneath the contour feathers, especially as an added insulation on water birds. There are also tiny hairlike feathers which lack barbs.

Feathers are the most salient characteristic of all birds. A birds' body is not totally covered with feathers, however, for they grow only in specific tracts, which are named according to the area of the body they occupy. When a bird is brooding her eggs she will wriggle as she sits down to bring one of the bare spots on her skin into contact with the eggs. This supplies the eggs with greater heat and also relieves the hen of uncomfortable heat which develops during brooding time.

The wing feathers can be distinguished from the tail feathers because the shaft of tail feathers is almost straight while on wing feathers it is distinctly curved; also the barbs on both sides of the shaft are of unequal length on wing feathers, the longer ones overlapping the shorter ones on the vane situated behind it on the wing. Thus the feathers lie one upon the other like the shingles on a roof. The tips or ends of the tail feathers are rounded or square in contrast to the pointed tips of wing feathers.

The wing is a most elegantly constructed organ. Each long feather is separately attached by a tendon to the bone and is thus maneuverable at various angles. This enables the bird to allow the air to go through the wing when desired or to tighten it up when air resistance is needed. Where the wing needs more thickness to allow the air to flow easily over and under it are three rows of short contour feathers called coverts. These are present both above and below the wing and serve also to close the gaps between the quills of neighboring feathers.

WHERE TO FIND THEM

Feathers are found anywhere birds come to ground—near a lake, on lawns, near beaches or other coastal areas where gulls rest, in or around aviaries or zoo cages, or in your own bird cage during moulting

CONTOUR FEATHER THAT FOLLOWS BODY FORM

DOWN FEATHER

FLIGHT FEATHER

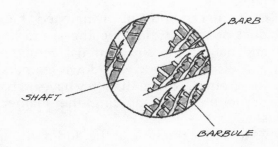

BARB

SHAFT

BARBULE

time. A boxful can usually be gotten from a poultry farm or various feathers can be purchased from an arts and crafts shop.

ACTIVITIES

1. Gather feathers on a trip to a lake or the seashore, or wherever many birds congregate.

2. Have the children run with a strong flight feather in the outstretched hands. They can notice the resistance such a feather offers to the wind. This will give them some idea of the strength of a feather.

3. Ruffle the feather until the barbs are unhooked, then smooth them out until the well-knit surface is restored.

4. Observe the barbs under a magnifying glass, both while they are hooked together and when separated. The stronger the magnification the more can be observed in this project. Maybe a binocular microscope can be borrowed on this occasion.

5. Make collections of feathers. Be sure you have contour feathers, the curved body feathers, the wing and tail feathers, and down. These can be kept in a book by sticking them on the page with cellophane tape.

6. If you can find a newly hatched chick or duck observe its down feathers, and stroke and handle the small animal gently. You may also be able to find down feathers on the ground. Notice that they have no barbs or central shaft holding the feather in shape.

7. Look for the hole at the end of the quill of a large feather. This is where the nourishment came to the growing feather.

It is now useless, for like our nails and hair, a feather once grown is no longer living tissue.

8. Bring in a parakeet or canary in a cage. Observe the wing feathers, tail feathers, and down shed by these birds. Observe the parts of the bird where each of these develop.

9. Bring a wing (unfeathered) of a chicken in and compare the bones of the bird's wing with those in our own arm. Notice that as in our arm there is an upper section, an elbow, two bones between the elbow and wrist. On a bird's hand all but the thumb bone are fused together.

10. Observe the thumb bone, called the alula, to which a tuft of feathers is attached in the live bird. This arrangement enables the bird to gain height by a current of air being forced between the tuft and the rest of the wing.

11. Put a drop or more of water on a feather and notice how it sheds moisture and stays dry.

12. Blow a down feather around, then a light contour feather, then a wing or tail feather and notice how each resists the wind and how each is carried along.

SOME HELPFUL MATERIALS

chicken wing
feathers, assorted
magnifying glasses
parakeet or canary in cage
water

KEY VOCABULARY FOR CHILDREN

 barbs
*contour feathers
*coverts
 down
 shafts

*Suggested for older children only

Bibliography

FOR ADULTS

Bosiger, E. and J. M. Guilcher *A Bird Is Born*, New York, Sterling Publishing Co., Inc., 1959.

Conklin, Gladys *If I Were a Bird*, New York, Holiday House, Inc., 1965.

Cosgrove, Margaret *Eggs and What Happens Inside Them*, New York, Dodd, Mead, & Co., 1966.

Evans, Howard E. *Wasp Farm*, Garden City, N.Y., Doubleday & Co., Inc., 1973.

Hillcourt, William H. *Fun with Nature Hobbies; A Cub Scout Project Book*, New York, G. P. Putnam's Sons, 1970.

McClung, Robert M. *Bees, Wasps and Hornets and How They Live*, New York, William Morrow & Co., Inc., 1971.

Murie, Olaus A. *Field Guide to Animal Tracks*, Houghton Mifflin Co., Boston, 1954.

Sawyer, Edmund J. *Homes for Wildlife*, 6th ed., Bloomfield Hills, Mich., Cranbrook Institute of Science, 1969.

Selsam, Millicent E. *All About Eggs*, Reading, Mass., Addison-Wesley Publishing Co., Inc., 1952.

Selsam, Millicent E. *Egg to Chick*, New York, Harper & Row Publishers, Inc., 1970.

Von Frisch, Karl *Ten Little Housemates*, The MacMillan Co., N.Y. 1960.

FOR CHILDREN

Eastman, P. D. *The Best Nest*, New York, Random House, Inc., 1968.

Gans, Roma *It's Nesting Time*, New York, Thomas Y. Crowell Co., 1964.

Garelick, May *What Makes a Bird a Bird?*, Chicago, Follett Publishing Co., 1969.

Georgiou, Constantine *Wait & See*, Irvington-on-Hudson, N.Y., Harvey House, Inc., 1962.

Selsam, Millicent E. *Tony's Birds*, New York, Harper & Row, Publishers Inc., 1961.

Shakelford, Nina and Gorden E. Burks, *Bird Nests*, Golden Press, New York, 1962.

Sterling, Dorothy *Insects and the Homes They Build*, Garden City, N.Y., Doubleday & Co., Inc., 1954.

5 Looking for Things in the Ground

Soil

Soil is composed of what is known as parent material, organic increment, water, and gases. The parent material consists of particles worn from rocks and is therefore mineral in content. The organic increment is formed of bits of decayed animal and vegetable matter such as the bodies of insects or other animals, bones, feathers, rotted leaves or wood, and roots of plants. The amount of water soil can hold depends on the relative amount of organic increment: the more organic matter the greater proportion of water soil can contain. The most important gas in soil is air.

Coarse soil is known as sand or gravel. Its particles can be distinguished with the naked eye and a fistful will crumble easily. Finer soil in which the particles stick together is known as a clayey soil, the particles being so small that they cannot be seen without the use of magnification. Silty soil, neither so coarse as sand nor so fine as clay, is known as loam.

The organic matter in the soil goes through a development as it lies on the ground. Litter is the name given to recently deposited material on the surface of the soil, which has not yet disintegrated. Beneath the litter is a zone of partly rotted material, called duff, and just below this we come upon well-rotted organic material known as leaf mold. At the bottom of these zones is an area of mineral soil.

A multitude of plants and animals live in the soil: bacteria, single-celled microscopic animals that feed on the bacteria, worms too small for our eyes, and the larger earthworms. Larger animals and birds too make burrows in the soil.

WHERE TO FIND IT

Procure soil from a number of places so that the various samples can be compared. Suggested spots for digging: under a tree or bush (do not brush away the surface litter), a bare spot near a stony cliff where the soil is composed largely of rocky bits, on a beach at the shoreward edge, from a garden bed, etc.

HOW TO KEEP IT

Place each sample in a different container. Cover the soil with plastic wrap to keep in moisture. However, once the soil is obtained the activities should not be postponed long enough to allow it to dry out.

ACTIVITIES

1. Examine each of the samples through a magnifying glass. See if the parent material and the organic increment can be distinguished. Rub some soil between thumb and finger to determine its texture—whether it is gritty or smooth. Notice if the soil is damp and observe the texture—whether the particles adhere, thus allowing little space between for air.

2. Test samples of soil to see if air is present. Fill a glass or plastic tumbler about 1 centimeter from the top with soil. Then, slowly pour water onto the soil. As the water soaks in it displaces air which bubbles to the top. The size and frequency of bubbles will give an idea of the amount of air the particular soil sample contains.

3. Try to make "snakes": Mix soil with a little water and mold into the shape of a hot-dog bun. Observe how the clayey samples make smooth "snakes," how the sandy samples cannot be rolled at all, while those formed of silt will be brittle.

4. Place samples of the soil on large sheets of wrapping paper and pick over each one (a team might be assigned to each sample). Make piles of such components as bits of stones, an ant's wing, a bit of crumbly soil, a partially rotted leaf, a feather, etc., and compare this organic increment from each pile.

5. Put a spoonful of soil in a jar of water, stir it, and watch the sediment settle to the bottom. Note that the material will sort itself out, the larger pieces below the smaller, lighter ones.

6. The children should attempt to mold the various textures of soil into shapes using various molding implements such as bowls, pans, cookie and gelatin molds. For smaller children, mud pies will demonstrate which sorts of soil retain the shape of the mold best.

7. Smell the soil when wet and when dry. This can be done outdoors after the rain and during a dry spell.

8. Place a sample of each soil in a flowerpot and water in order to observe the sprouting weed seeds. These have lain dormant when the ground was dry and will be more plentiful in some soils than in others.

9. Plant the same variety of quickly sprouting seeds, such as beans, in flowerpots filled with the various samples of soil. Place the pots near each other so that they are exposed to the same conditions. Places

selected could be near a sunny window, near the heater, or in a cool, shady spot, either indoors or out. Water regularly and observe in which soil the seeds thrive best.

THIS IS AN ACTIVITY SUITABLE FOR OLDER CHILDREN AND THE PROCEDURES SHOULD BE CARRIED ON BY THE CHILDREN THEMSELVES.

SOME HELPFUL MATERIALS

containers for keeping soil
flowerpots
magnifying glasses
newspapers or large sheets of
  wrapping paper
plastic wrap
seeds, quick sprouting, such as beans
soil from various places
Styrofoam or plastic tumblers

KEY VOCABULARY FOR CHILDREN

  air
  clay
  gravel
  gritty
  loam
*mineral
*organic
  sand
  silt
  soil

*Suggested for older children only

Sand

Sand is composed of bits of many different materials. Some are derived from broken rocks, others from shells or other organic materials such as dried seaweed, crab claws, etc. Some sand may have come from the cliffs on an adjacent shore, having been deposited underneath the water. Some may have been carried by rivers running to the sea or by winds blowing from dry places. Fine sand on the desert is mostly windborne and coarse sand on the beach is likely to have arrived there by an agent with greater carrying power, such as the ocean itself or the rivers that run into it. And because of the many places where it may have come from, sand found on one beach or in the bed of one stream may differ drastically from that found on another, even one not far distant.

Sands are of many different textures, some being almost as fine as dust while others are so coarse that the single grains can be picked up with the fingers. This coarse sand grades from gravel into silt, where the grains become almost too fine to be separated by the eye.

The colors of sand also differ because of the source of the sand. If formed from disintegrated rock, for instance, the particles will resemble those in the original rock and will sometimes include bits of black mica, quartz, and feldspar. Depending on the color of the feldspar, which is the predominant mineral in granite, the sand may take on a pinkish, white, or yellow color. The mica bits may be black and shiny or colorless and iridescent, and the quartz is glassy and apt to remain after the other minerals have been ground to dust, for quartz is a hard mineral. Brown sand may be the result of broken-down sandstone and may be so claylike in texture that the bits will stick together.

Larger-grained sands often come to rest on steeply sloping dunes. Here the larger grains, frequently with rough edges, are caught and hold fast to each other at what is known as the angle of repose.

Mixed with some sands there may be black particles of magnetite. This material, known as lodestone, is magnetic and can be gathered by drawing a magnet through the sand. However, not all black sand is magnetite, some is composed of volcanic materials as in Hawaii, in the Northwest, and on some South Pacific beaches.

WHERE TO FIND SAND

Sand may be found primarily on a beach, but if you are not near a beach sand may be found in a stream bed or the sand in the sandbox can be used for this project. However, sand box sand has been strained and will yield a smaller amount and variation of materials. Several kinds of sand are usually available in hardware or building supplies stores.

ACTIVITIES

1. Strain the sand through a coarse strainer and then through a fine one. Examine each of the siftings as well as what remains in the strainer with a magnifying glass and see if the differently colored grains can be distinguished (some of them look like jewels). Notice that the edges of some grains have been worn smooth and those of others are still sharp. This indicates the hardness of the material of which they are formed and how well they have been able to resist erosion.

2. Place a spoonful of sand in a mason jar filled with water, screw on the top, and shake well. Notice which grains float. Some of these will probably be pieces of plants, wood, or other very light materials. Watch how the sediment finally settles and how it is sorted by size, the heavier pieces and the larger ones being at the bottom.

3. Make a ball of wet sand and allow it to dry. How long will it hold together? If it can do so for a fairly long time there are likely to be clay particles among the grains of sand, which came from the breakdown of clays washed down from adjacent cliffs or brought down by rivers from similar formations farther inland. Very fine sand may possibly contain a great deal of this sticky clay and when wet will hold the water so that it is shiny after being doused with water. Clay sands will clump and shrink when dry and can then be broken up into large lumps. Ground largely composed of clay will split into cracks when dry.

4. Run a magnet through sand containing a great many black grains. If these grains adhere to the magnet they are magnetite. Gather this up and place on a piece of paper. Then hold a magnet underneath the paper, moving it about. The sand grains will follow its movements. Now place the magnet under some clear paper and sprinkle the magnetite on top of it. Notice how the two ends of the magnet, the poles, attract the grains so that the form of the magnet is outlined on the paper.

5. Let the children use wet sand for modeling and building.

6. Smooth some wet sand with a board and let the children model it in relief or draw pictures on it.

SOME HELPFUL MATERIALS

boards, wooden
jars, with screw-on lids
magnets
magnifying glasses
paper, news or wrapping
spoons
strainer, coarse
strainer, fine

KEY VOCABULARY FOR CHILDREN

erosion
grains
gravel
magnet
*magnetite
*sediment
silt

*Suggested for older children only

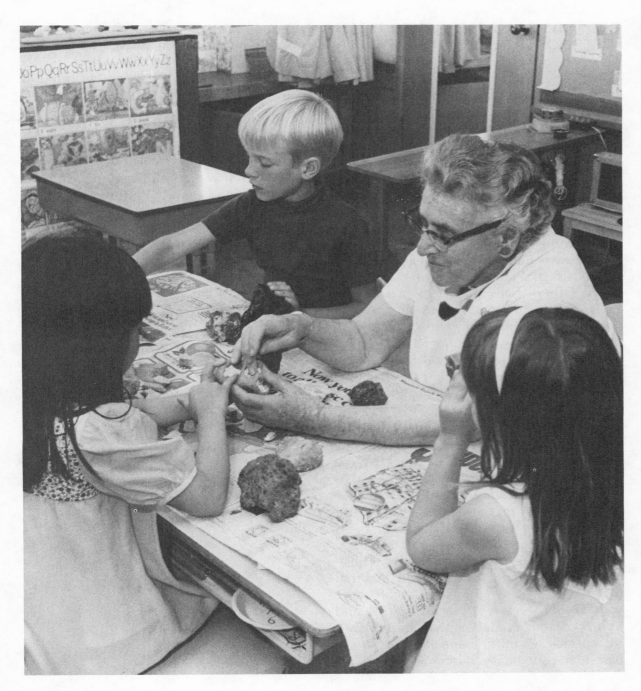

Rocks
and Pebbles

THE ACTIVIES IN THIS CHAPTER ARE BEST SUITED FOR OLDER CHILDREN.

Rocks, which are found almost everywhere, can tell us some sort of a story about themselves. We look for the cliff from which they may have broken off and if the rocks have sharp, unworn edges we known that their place of origin is near at hand. Their edges would have been worn smooth if they had been carried some distance from where they broke off. Rounded pebbles are known as water-worn. Some of these have only two sides worn down and flattened. These have been shaped in this manner by the surf which pushed them back and forth across the sands, turning them over from time to time and thus smoothing only two surfaces. The rounded pebbles worn on all sides have been tumbled down the bed of a rushing stream, where they were knocked against boulders and against rocks in motion like themselves.

Rocks have different textures. Some are gritty, indicating that they were formed by sedimentation of grains of sand. These are the sandstones. The mudstones, also sedimentary, are smooth and have smaller particles. The metamorphic rocks—the slates, shales, and marble, have been changed by heat or pressure or by both. Finally there are the igneous rocks. These have been formed from molten material under the surface of the earth, some being thrown out as lava from volcanoes and others having cooled slowly underneath the surface. Granite, a speckled rock, and basalt, a very heavy dark rock, are both igneous rocks. There are also man-made rocks—concrete, asphalt used for paving, and bricks.

Hard or well consolidated rocks differ in many ways. Some of them can be scratched with a knife and others are so hard that the steel of the knife is left on them when one attempts to scratch them. Such rocks are actually minerals, in which case they are composed of a single substance that can be described by a chemical formula. A rock, on

A GRANITIC ROCK

the other hand, is composed of two or more minerals.

Some rocks such as pumice can float; some, like coal, will burn and others will change their texture if subjected to heat.

ACTIVITIES

1. With a hammer, break off rocks from a cliff and examine the surface that has not been exposed to weather. To find such a specimen it is necessary to avoid breaking

FOSSIL SHELL IMBEDDED IN ROCK

off a rock that has a crack behind it that may have admitted water or air. Compare all sides of the rock.

2. Notice if the rock contains bits of differently formed and colored materials. Notice the size of these bits and how many varieties there are. Repeat this examination with a magnifying glass to reveal how many different varieties of minerals you can find in the granite.

3. Examine water-worn pebbles and note both with and without the magnifying glass whether they too have inclusions. Shells or broken bits of them are sometimes found embedded in surf-worn pebbles. These may be fossils.

4. Examine rocks that break up in the hand. Some of these are made of claylike materials, which when wet can be molded in the hands and allowed to dry in the sun to reform them into rock. If the clay were baked in the oven they would be even stronger.

5. Rocks that have not yet become hardened can sometimes be cut with a knife, so that it may be possible to carve them or if they are made of clay to model with them.

6. Make a collection of rocks. After picking them up wash them thoroughly so that their surface colors are revealed, then smash or crack others of the same variety (picked up from the same source), and compare the color of the outer surface with that of the unexposed portion.

7. Go on rock hunts, not forgetting to look for man-made as well as natural rocks.

8. Put the rocks on display and have the children explain to their parents or other children something about the exhibits.

SOME HELPFUL MATERIALS

*containers for collecting rocks
    (egg boxes are handy for displaying)*
fossil
granite samples
hammers
magnifying glasses
sandstone
slate or marble

KEY VOCABULARY FOR CHILDREN

claylike
fossils
minerals
mudstones
pebbles
sandstone
water-worn

Earthworms

The earthworm belongs to a group of animals having segmented bodies. Each segment contains the same structures, with two exceptions, the head and clitellum. The mouth is on the head, but there are no eyes. The earthworm, which burrows underground, has little or no need of them. The clitellum is the swollen ring extending from about the 31st to the 37th segment of the body. It contains a great many glands which secrete mucus to form the walls of a cocoon in which the eggs and sperm are laid and where fertilization takes place. After fertilization the oval cocoon slips over the head of the earthworm and remains in the soil until the eggs hatch. Earthworms are bisexual, each individual possessing both male and female organs, each of which contributes to the contents of the cocoon.

As earthworms have no legs locomotion is effected by extending the forepart of the body, then anchoring it by means of hairlike structures on the underside (setae), and finally contracting or pulling up the rear portion of the body.

Earthworms construct their burrows by swallowing soil as they move along and depositing it mixed with mucus along the sides of the burrow. Some of the excess dirt may sometimes be found on the surface of the ground in the form of castings.

WHERE TO FIND THEM

Turn over a shovelful of dirt in a damp spot, under a tree, or in a cultivated garden. The younger, smaller earthworms will be near the surface and the larger ones may be come upon as deep as a meter or more underground. They may also be gathered by strewing some of the food mentioned below on a lawn and covering it with a piece of burlap. The earthworms will come out to feed on it.

HOW TO CARE FOR THEM

Keep the worms in a large box made of some material that will not deteriorate when wet. Fill the box to a depth of about 10 cm (4 inches) with soil mixed with peat moss. Keep this well watered but not waterlogged. Place a cover over the box.

WHAT TO FEED THEM

Feed with grass cuttings, corn meal, or bits of food from the table. Place this on top of the soil and cover with a fresh layer of soil every few days, the whole to be kept damp.

ACTIVITIES

1. Let the children dig the worms outside with which to stock their "worm castle."
2. From time to time dump the contents of the box on a large sheet of heavy paper to observe the worms, to handle them, and to find cocoons or young worms.
3. Observe an earthworm under a magnifying glass and locate the setae on the underside by which the animal anchors itself as it pulls its body forward. Place the earthworms on a smooth or glass surface and determine whether they can move without gripping a rough surface.
4. Find the head and note the absence of eyes. Find the mouth just behind the first segment and try to feed the animal. (It is

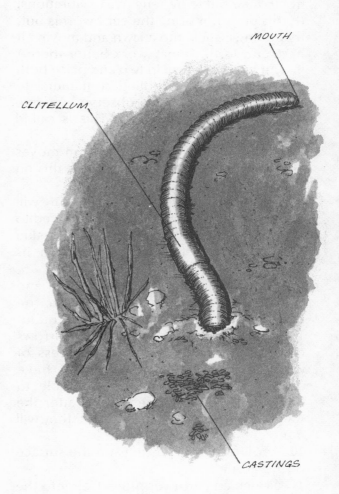

MOUTH

CLITELLUM

CASTINGS

nocturnal and will probably not eat from your hand during the day.) Locate the clitellum.

5. Drive a stick into the soil of the box and move it sharply to and fro. The vibrations set up in the ground should bring the earthworms to the surface. Worms are said not to hear but to be sensitive to vibrations. (If this does not bring the earthworms out, try driving a stick into a lawn and moving it back and forth. It may work better there.)

6. Cut an earthworm in two and place both parts in separate dirt-filled containers. In time you will be able to observe how one piece will grow a new tail. This is called regeneration.

7. Observe the way an earthworm moves along and have the children mimic this on the floor.

8. Touch the earthworm and you will notice that the body is moist. If allowed to dry out the earthworm will die. (It has a skin that allows moisture to escape from its body.)

9. After a rainy spell go outside and observe earthworms stranded on the pavement or the surface of the ground. They have emerged from their burrows during the rain because of an excess of water which might otherwise have drowned them. Unless they are able to burrow quickly into the ground after the rain stops and before they dry out, they will die.

10. Look for worm castings on the surface of the ground.

11. Watch an earthworm dig itself into the loose soil.

12. Observe a robin on a lawn and notice how motionless it stands (freezing, it is called) while trying to locate an earthworm below the surface. Some say the bird sees the grass moving as the worm crawls among the roots, others claims that the bird feels the movement of the grass roots, and still others believe that the bird can hear the worm moving underneath the ground. In any case you will observe that the bird nearly always gets its prey. The interdependence of all animals might be taken up at this point, explaining that one animal is dependent upon another, which in turn is dependent upon something else, animal or plant life. The predators are not *bad* and the victims are not the "good guys."

13. Let the children play at being robins picking up worms.

SOME HELPFUL MATERIALS

boxes with covers
burlap
glass, panes
grass cuttings
magnifying glasses
paper, wrapping
peat moss
scissors
shovels
soil from damp area
sticks

KEY VOCABULARY FOR CHILDREN

bristles
burrows
castings
*cocoon
*segments

*Suggested for older children only

Sowbugs
and Pillbugs

SOWBUG

Because both sowbugs and pillbugs are quite common in many localities, they have received many local names, such as little pigs of the woods and little asses, the latter because of their grey color. They are not insects, but like the insects they belong to the larger group called arthropods, meaning "jointed legs." Like insects, they have segmented bodies and an outer skeleton to which the muscles are attached on the inner surface. Sowbugs and pillbugs are crustaceans, cousins to crabs and lobsters, having more than six legs, two or more antennae, and very complicated mouthparts.

A pillbug can be distinguished from a sowbug by its ability to roll itself into a ball (or pill) for protection. The sowbug in such circumstances can only scurry out of harm's way as fast as its seven pairs of legs will carry it. Both animals have a pouch on the under-surface of the body near the rear end, where the eggs are deposited. When the young hatch, white and almost transparent, they remain in the pouch for a while, only leaving it when they are large enough to fend for themselves. They breed from March to October.

Overlapping scales cover the body of these crustaceans. Except for the five front scales, the head, the two rear ones, and the tail, these scales are flexible, giving the body freedom of movement.

WHERE TO FIND THEM

Look for sowbugs and pillbugs in damp places, underneath rocks or boards or in piles of damp rubbish. Because they

PILLBUG

breathe by means of gills they cannot live in dry places.

HOW TO CARE FOR THEM

Place them in a box or other container the floor of which is covered with some of the soil from the spot where they were found. A small, flat board or a rock should be laid lightly on this ground so that the animals are able to crawl underneath. Keep the ground damp but not wet or you will force the animals to seek a drier shelter.

WHAT TO FEED THEM

Sowbugs and pillbugs are herbivorous. They eat leaves, both soft green ones and decayed ones. These must be placed on the ground and kept moist by sprinkling with water. The leaves should be placed a short distance from the hiding place to encourage the animals to come out to feed.

ACTIVITIES

1. Try to find both pillbugs and sowbugs and notice the way one runs away and the other rolls up for protection.

2. The upper and undersides of the body differ, the upper being covered with hard-shelled scales and the under being soft. Examine them and feel them both. Look for the short feelers, or antennae, and watch how the animals manipulate them.

3. Watch them dig themselves into the soil under the protection of the rock or board.

4. Look for the animals outside and bring them inside, along with the soil for the box and the rotted leaves or other food.

5. The children should be allowed to sprinkle the soil with a light spray after determining whether it needs moisture by feeling it.

6. Observe the animals under a magnifying glass and try to locate the mouth, eyes, tail, scales, etc.

7. Watch them eating and notice how the legs are used to pick up food.

8. Allow them to crawl over the children's hands and notice that though the legs of both sowbugs and pillbugs are without claws or sharp tips, even so they are able to cling when held upside down.

9. Turn the sowbugs on their backs and watch how the legs are used to right themselves.

SOME HELPFUL MATERIALS

board, flat, wooden
boxes, wooden or plastic
soil
watering can

KEY VOCABULARY FOR CHILDREN

feelers
gills
scales

Centipedes
and Millipedes

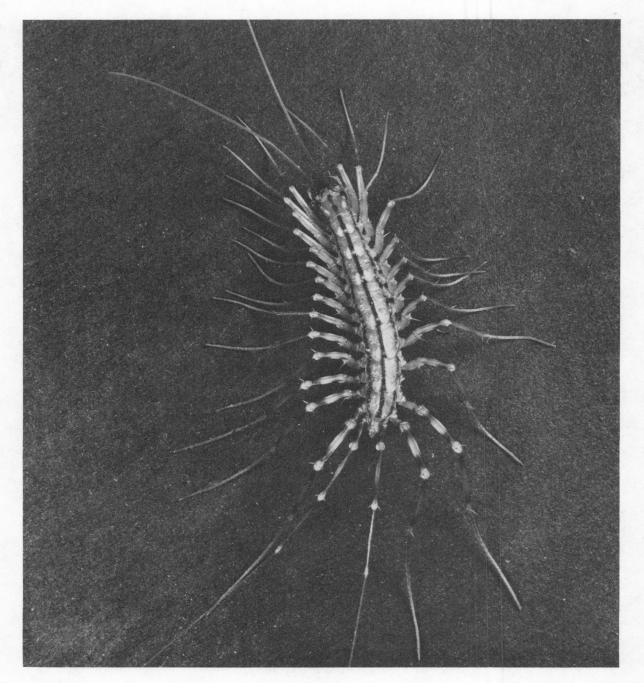

Centipedes and millipedes belong to that group of animals known as arthropods, or animals with jointed legs. Insects, crustaceans, and sowbugs and pillbugs also belong to this group. All arthropods are characterized not only by jointed legs but also by an exoskeleton covering the body parts and giving them support.

Centipedes and millipedes have segmented bodies and are secretive animals, living in dark places such as beneath leaf mold, in the soil, or underneath stones or wood. They have a pair of antennae and in most cases eye spots which are sensitive only to light and dark. The mouth is the underside of the head facing the ground.

Centipedes and millipedes are often confused with one another though they are easily distinguished. The centipede has a flattened body and one pair of legs attached to each segment. Though the word *centipede* means 100 legs, most varieties average about 35 pairs, which enable them to move swiftly to safety and to squirm in a lively manner. The centipede is sensitive to strong light and is therefore found only in dark places. Our most common variety of centipede lays its eggs in the ground or in a hollow, rotten log, the mother curling herself around her eggs and the young, when they first hatch, so as to protect them until they are large enough to look out for themselves.

In contrast to the centipede the millipede is a sluggish animal. It is often found curled up in a spiral. Its name is also a misnomer for it possesses far less than a thousand legs. It has two pairs of legs on each segment. Like the centipede the millipede has a hard, shell-like covering made of chiton, the same material that covers the bodies of insects. Both also have a pair of antennae and the millipede also shuns the light and seeks out damp, dark spots.

Neither of these animals is poisonous. It is merely a legend that the centipede of the desert can poison people. Both of these organisms can be safely handled by the children.

WHERE TO FIND THEM

Look for centipedes in a damp place underneath large rocks, dead leaves, or boards lying on the ground. A certain variety of centipede with long, striped legs and a very long pair of antennae is sometimes trapped in bathtubs. Millipedes are also found in damp soil or in rotting wood, under leaves and stones, and in the bark of trees.

HOW TO CARE FOR THEM

Place about 5 cm (2 inches) of soil in a water-tight container of about 30 cm (a foot) or more in length. The ground must be throughly watered but never soggy. A board or rock should be placed lightly on the surface of the ground so that the animal may have a place in which to hide from the light and where it is protected from drying out. Though it is necessary to keep the soil wet, if it is too wet millipedes will seek a drier spot. DO NOT KEEP CENTIPEDES AND MILLIPEDES IN THE SAME CONTAINER! Millipedes emit a gas which is poisonous to centipedes and may kill them.

CENTIPEDE

MILLIPEDE

121

WHAT TO FEED THEM

A centipede is carnivorous and has a pair of poison glands on the first pair of legs, but this poison is of such a mild variety that it cannot harm even a small child. It is used, however, to kill small insects, such as cockroaches and aphids, and also earthworms and slugs. The centipede should be fed such animals as these.

A millipede, on the other hand, is herbivorous and feeds only on decaying plant food such as rotting leaves, roots, and very tender leaves.

ACTIVITIES

1. Find centipedes or millipedes and compare them, noting the number of legs on each segment of the body, which is the best way to distinguish the two. The centipede is the wriggler but the millipede will coil and uncoil its body if it is disturbed.
2. Prepare the containers for these animals. A terrarium may be used or a wooden or plastic box, the first made waterproof with foil both inside and out.
3. After placing food in the container watch the animals eat.
4. Observe them under a magnifying glass and see if the eyespots and mouth can be located.
5. Observe the undulating motion of the legs as those in the front of the body move first, followed by those behind them, then the legs on one side and then on the other.
6. Millipedes give off a distinct odor. Have the children smell them.
7. Draw, paint, or model in clay these insects.

SOME HELPFUL MATERIALS

board, flat, wooden
container, water-tight
magnifying glasses
terrarium

KEY VOCABULARY FOR CHILDREN

*antennae
coil
eyespots
leaf mold
*uncoil

*Suggested for older children only

EGGS

PUPAE

LARVAE

ADULT

Ants have an exoskeleton, six legs, three parts to the body and antennae, which serve as organs of touch and smell. Most ants have compound eyes made up of six-sided lenses. Ants have complicated mouthparts useful for carrying, digging, building, grasping, and fighting as well as for chewing up their food. One part of the mouth also serves as a comb and cleaner for the long antennae. The head is of course the first of the three parts of the body. To the thorax are attached the legs and wings, if present. Between the thorax and the abdomen, is a tiny button-shaped organ by which an ant can be distinguished from other insects.

Ants go through a complete metamorphosis. From their very small eggs hatch legless grubs, or larvae, which are fed by adult ants. In time these larvae change into pupae resembling tiny, elongated bundles. It is these pupae that the adult ants carry to safety when danger threatens the anthill.

Winged ants are the males and females whose wings carry them aloft to mate in the air. The mating completed, the male dies and the female returns to the ground, tears off her now useless wings and finds a spot in which to lay her eggs.

The first larvae to hatch are fed by the queen from food stored in her own body and derived for the most part from the muscles that once operated the wings. When this first brood has completed its metamorphosis from pupae to full-grown ants, the queen retires to a life of egg laying, leaving the feeding and rearing of the young to the other adult ants.

WHERE TO FIND THEM

Follow an ant trail either outdoors or one that leads into the house until you come upon a hole in the ground or other evidence of an ant colony. Anthills are found in dry places where the soil is loose and easily dug into. Sometimes ants will nest in rotting logs, even in cracks in cement and in many other unlikely spots.

HOW TO HOUSE THEM

"Ant palaces" or "ant farms" may be purchased. These are composed of two panes of glass securely fastened in a frame which is attached in an upright position to a base. The space between the two panes is filled with pulverized soil. An opening with a cover for the insertion of food is located at the top. In addition to this opening there is another in which a small sponge has been placed. This is kept moist and is the source of water for the ants. A cover for the whole container is also furnished in this kit and ants may be purchased to stock it.

It isn't necessary to buy a commercial product, though. An ant farm can easily be constructed by placing a shallow baking pan inside a larger one. This large outer pan is kept filled with water to prevent ants from escaping. Over the inner pan is placed a pane of glass, which must not extend beyond or touch the outer pan. SAFETY NOTE: *Tape any sharp edges on the glass.* The inner pan is then filled with soil and a shovelful of ants added. The queen ant must be included or else the colony will soon die out. She is distinguished by being much larger than the other ants. It is essential to keep a dark covering over the ant colony at all times, except when observing the ants. Otherwise they will burrow down or become inactive.

WHAT TO FEED THEM

Feed ants a drop of honey mixed with water, a crumb or two of bread, an ant-sized piece of meat or fish, a dead fly, or one or two bird seeds. Don't overfeed or the food will rot or mildew. If this happens remove it with a forceps. A tiny sponge, kept damp, should also be placed in the ant palace.

ACTIVITIES

1. Let the children track down an anthill and poke into it with a stick. They will be able to observe how the disturbed ants bring out the pupae. By watching quietly the children can observe how long it takes before the ants return to the nest with their burdens.

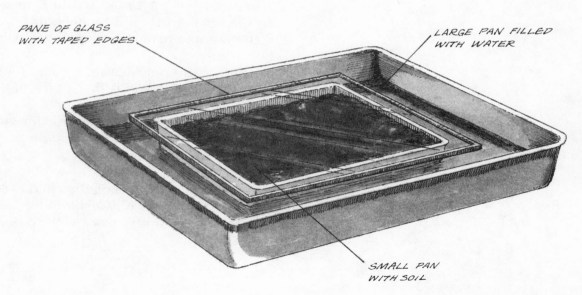

PANE OF GLASS WITH TAPED EDGES

LARGE PAN FILLED WITH WATER

SMALL PAN WITH SOIL

2. Place an obstacle in the path of an ant and observe how it gets around the obstacle.

3. Place a dead fly or other food in the ant's pathway and watch how the ant will carry it away to the nest. See if it goes for help and if so notice how one ant communicates with another by means of its antennae.

4. Look for different varieties of ants—the tiny Argentine ant that invades our homes and the much larger black or red ants. (The latter may bite although ant bites are not dangerous, except for those of certain tropical species.) Don't place more than one species of ants in the same container, lest one exterminate the other.

5. The children can help to dig out the ants for their home-made ant palace.

6. Once the ants are established in the container remove the covering from time to time to observe how they tunnel through the soil; look for the chambers the ants have hollowed out for the eggs and pupae.

7. The children should be encouraged to feed the ants and to keep the sponge damp (not wet).

8. Hold an ant between thumb and finger and sniff. Formic acid is the source of this smell.

9. Observe an ant under a magnifying glass and locate the eyes, mouth, and the many segments of the antennae.

10. Play a game of follow-the-leader, pretending to be ants, feeling the child ahead and behind instead of watching him. This can be done in a safe place with the eyes blindfolded.

SOME HELPFUL MATERIALS

"ant palace" or pans, shallow
ants
glass, panes (edges taped)
magnifying glasses
soil
sponge, small
sticks

KEY VOCABULARY FOR CHILDREN

"ant palace"
*antennae
feelers
females
grubs
males
queen
*thorax

*Suggested for older children only

Bibliography

FOR ADULTS

Bartlett, Margaret F. *Down the Mountain; A Book About the Ever-Changing Soil,* Reading, Mass., Addison-Wesley Publishing Co., Inc., 1963.

Bartlett, Ruth *Insect Engineers: The Story of Ants,* New York, William Morrow & Co., Inc., 1957.

Centipedes and Millipedes—Leaflet #192, U.S. Dept. of Agriculture, Superintendent of Documents, U.S. Gov't Printing Office, Washington D.C. 20025.

Gans, Roma *The Wonder of Stones,* New York, Thomas Y. Crowell Co., 1963.

George, Jean Craighead *All Upon a Stone,* New York, Thomas Y. Crowell Co., 1971.

Keene, Melvin *The Beginners' Story of Minerals and Rocks,* New York, Harper & Row Publishers, Inc., 1966.

Mitchell, Arthur A. *First Aid to Insects and Much More,* Irvington-On-Hudson, N.Y., Harvey House, Inc., 1964.

Podendorf, Illa *The True Book of Rocks and Minerals,* Chicago, Children's Press, 1972.

Schneider, Herman and Nina Schneider *Rocks, Rivers & The Changing Earth,* Reading, Mass., Addison-Wesley Publishing Co., Inc., 1952.

Schoenknecht, Charles A. *Ants,* Chicago, Follett Publishing Co., 1961.

Shuttlesworth, Dorothy E. *The Story Of Ants,* Garden City, N.Y., Doubleday & Co., Inc., 1964.

Simon, Seymour *Discovering what Earthworms Do,* New York, McGraw-Hill Book Co., 1969.

Vevers, Henry Gwynne *Ants and Termites,* New York, McGraw-Hill Book Co., 1966.

Wyler, Rose and Gerald Ames *Secrets in Stone,* New York, Four Winds Press, 1970.

Zim, Herbert S. and Paul R. Shaffer, *Rocks and Minerals,* New York, Western Publishing Co., Inc., 1957.

FOR CHILDREN

Branley, Franklin M. *Big Tracks Little Tracts,* New York, Thomas Y. Crowell, Co., 1960.

Conklin, Gladys *We Like Bugs,* New York, Holiday House, Inc., 1962.

Huntington, Harriet E. *Let's Go to the Brook,* Garden City, N.Y., Doubleday & Co., Inc., 1952.

Huntington, Harriet E. *Let's Go to the Desert,* Garden City, N.Y., Doubleday & Co., Inc., 1949.

Myrick, Mildred *Ants Are Fun,* New York, Harper & Row, Publishers Inc., 1968.

Podendorf, Illa *The True Book of Insects,* Chicago Children's Press, 1972.

Selsam, Millicent E. *Terry and the Caterpillars,* New York, Harper & Row Publishers, 1962.

Syrocki, B. John *What Is Soil?,* Westchester, Ill., Benefic Press, 1961.

6 Projects with Plants

CROWN

TRUNK

ROOTS

THE ACTIVITIES IN THIS PROJECT ARE BEST SUITED FOR OLDER CHILDREN.

There are many varieties of trees and those that are accessible to any particular school area may be quite different from those found in another. Therefore it would be impossible to give here a specific description of "your" tree. However, there are certain characteristics that apply to any tree, for every tree is composed of three parts—roots, trunk, and crown.

The roots serve to transport moisture and dissolved minerals from the soil to the trunk. Because roots are as extensive as the part of the tree above ground, they are able to give the tree firm anchorage. In addition, the roots of dormant trees store food.

Within the trunk of a tree are tubes that transport moisture from the roots upward and others that carry down the food formed in the leaves. The trunk is composed of a number of layers. The bark on the outside is dead material and between it and the wood is a living zone known as the cambium layer. Here new wood is formed and added to the core of the tree. The sapwood is underneath the cambium layer and at the center of the tree is the heartwood, no longer living but furnishing strong support to the trunk. Through the sapwood run the tubes for carrying moisture and food. Each year a new layer of wood is added to the outer surface of the sapwood, thus forming the annual growth rings by which the age of a tree can be determined. The wider the ring the more favorable the season has been for growth. The trunk of a tree also supports the crown, raising it aloft where

the leaves are within reach of the sunlight that provides the energy to manufacture food for the tree.

All trees bear flowers, which are usually inconspicuous unless they depend on insects or birds for fertilization. For many trees the wind is the agent for distributing pollen and therefore such trees must produce an abundance of this male substance, much of which necessarily goes to waste. (See Flowers, page 139.)

Cone-bearing trees are among those that have two sorts of flowers, male and female. The male flowers produce the pollen and the female flowers, usually found high above the ground out of harm's way, contain the potential seeds.

ACTIVITIES

1. A tree can and should be observed at all seasons of the year. If it is deciduous the falling leaves can be collected, preserved,

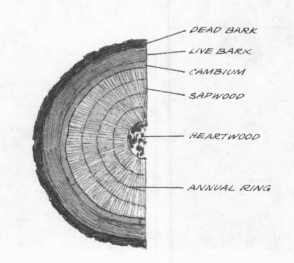

DEAD BARK
LIVE BARK
CAMBIUM
SAPWOOD
HEARTWOOD
ANNUAL RING

or prints made of them (see Leaves, pages 135–137). If the tree is evergreen, the leaves, or "needles", should be examined as to why they are able to withstand cold and rain. Are they protected by a sort of varnish? Are they very small and narrow so that they cannot support a blanket of snow?

2. Look for the leaf buds at the place where the leaf stem meets the twig. (see Bare Twigs, pages 132–135). Cut off the two leaf buds and carefully slit lengthwise with a knife, then crosswise, to reveal the tiny leaves folded inside.

3. Some of the leaf buds may contain flowers instead of leaves. Examine them and compare both sorts.

4. Examine the leaf stem. Roll it between the fingers to determine the shape—round, flattened, angled, etc. Notice how the leaf stem is attached to the leaf and to the twig upon which it grows. Also, observe the leaf bud between the leaf stem and the twig. Look for the leaf scar left by the stem of last year's fallen leaf.

5. Observe the arrangement of the leaves along the twig. Are they opposite one another, as on the maple tree, alternate as on sycamores and apple trees, or are there several growing around the stem from the same node, as on the oleander? (See Leaves, pages 135–137.)

6. Is the leaf a needle type? Is it like a true needle as on pine trees, awl-shaped as on the Norfolk Island pine and some junipers, or scalelike as on the cypresses?

7. Look for the seeds of the tree. In cone-bearing trees they are at the base of the bracts inside the cone.

8. Plant some of the seeds indoors.

9. Feel the bark of the tree and notice its texture—rough, smooth, scaly, furrowed, etc.

12. How does the dead bark allow for expansion of the tree's girth?—By splitting, peeling off, furrowing, etc?

10. What is the shape of the tree as a whole, its silhouette? Make a drawing of the tree's outline and compare it with the outline of another tree.

11. How high above the ground does the bare trunk extend? Does the trunk divide and if so, at what height?

12. Examine the stumps of a large and a small tree. Count the annual growth rings on each to determine its age when cut down. Identify the heartwood, cambium layer, sapwood, and bark.

13. If you can find an uprooted tree, observe the roots and notice how they are spread out and taper toward to tips.

SOME HELPFUL MATERIALS

fallen leaves
knife
magnifying glasses
pruning saw
pruning shears

KEY VOCABULARY FOR CHILDREN

bark
cambium
cones
crown
growth rings
heartwood
roots
sapwood
trunk

PINE
(NEEDLE SHAPED)

CYPRESS
(SCALELIKE)

JUNIPER
(AWL SHAPED)

Bare Twigs

A twig has swellings on it called nodes. Its age can be determined by counting the number of nodes below the terminal bud (the one at the end), each node indicating a year's growth. At each node there is a leaf scar whose shape varies with every species of plant. On the leaf scar are tiny dots, the remains of the tubes that once carried the sap from the roots to the leaf and the food from the leaf to the other parts of the plant. Just above the leaf scar on many plants is a leaf bud. In winter this is a tightly wrapped bundle protected from wind and weather either with a heavy, varnished shell or with a wooly or hairy one.

Inside the bud are tiny leaves or flowers folded neatly away. They will remain dormant until the sap starts flowing from the roots in spring, when they start to expand and burst out of the shell that contained them. The leaf buds are arranged in one of three ways on the stem—opposite one another at the same node, on alternate nodes, or several growing out from all sides of a node. On a twig that is cut cleanly across, the rings of growth inside can be counted. (You may need a magnifying glass for this.) The thickness of the protecting bark, the heartwood, and sapwood may also be observed in the same cut (see A Tree, pages 129–131).

Another set of twigs should be examined later in the year when the plant is in leaf. New leaf buds, nestling in the angle between the leaf stem and the twig (axil), will have grown out, as the leaf burst from its winter covering. The leaf scars of previous years will still be visible and if a green leaf is broken off at the base of its

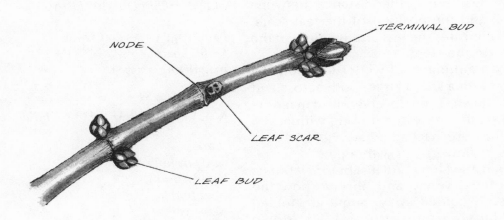

stem, this attachment to the twig can be observed and sap may run out of it.

WHERE TO FIND THEM

Look for bare twigs wherever plants are growing. The dry twigs on deciduous trees may still be living tissue, but those found on evergreens are most likely dead. Also pick some twigs from shrubs and flowering plants. Even though these may not be bare, certain of the characteristics noted above will be identifiable.

ACTIVITIES

1. Place a bare twig in a container of water and watch the leafbuds open. This may take some time but in most cases the buds will sprout in a warm room.
2. Make drawings of the "little faces" formed by the leaf scars. Do this with a number of different trees and shrubs.
3. Make a collection of twigs. Notice the differences between the bark, the position

of the leaf buds, the distance between nodes, and the position of the leaf scars, which indicates the leaf arrangement of the leaves on the stem.

4. Open a number of winter leaf buds by cutting with a sharp knife, both across and up and down. Then observe with a magnifying glass the leaves or flowers within and how they are packed away. Pick the tiny leaves or flowers out with a pin.

5. Open a swelling bud just before it bursts its winter covering and observe how the leaves are folded away. Some are folded like fans, some are folded down lengthwise, some are folded crosswise, some are arranged in a sort of cone, and others are packed neatly side by side. This is best observed in a large leaf bud such as that of a horse chestnut.

6. Feel the texture of the surface of the leaf buds.

7. Make drawings of leaf buds and of twigs.

SOME HELPFUL MATERIALS

bare twigs of several kinds
knife, sharp
magnifying glasses

KEY VOCABULARY FOR CHILDREN

bark
growth rings
*heartwood
leaf bud
leaf scar
node
*sapwood

*Suggested for older children only

Leaves are very important plant organs because they contain the substance called chlorophyll, which, in the presence of sunlight, can convert carbon dioxide from the air and water from the ground into food. Every living thing on earth, plant or animal, derives its food directly or indirectly from this process, called photosynthesis, which takes place in the leaf.

Leaves are of many shapes, textures, and colors, which enable them to adapt to many different environments. Some leaves are covered with protective tissues to keep them from freezing or from drying out, some, such as the succulents, can store water. Others, such as cactus "spines", are reduced in size to conserve water, so that they are hardly recognizable as leaves at all.

The edges of leaves are also variously adapted, in some cases for withstanding winds that might tear them to pieces and in others for protecting them against browsing animals. Some leaves are unpalatable and others are spiny or sharp-edged. Leaves growing in full sunshine may be slender; those in shady places are apt to be wide and flat—able to catch as much sunlight as possible. Some leaves are rigidly attached to their stems and others tremble at the slightest breeze.

At regular intervals along the stalk of a plant there are nodes from which the leaves grow. In some plants two or more leaves grow from the same node on opposite sides of the stem, and in others only one leaf grows at each node, springing alternately from the opposite sides of the stem.

Each of these arrangements prevents a leaf growing above from casting a shadow on those below. Also at the node, between the stem of the leaf and the main stalk, is a leaf bud which grows into a new leaf if the present leaf is injured or destroyed. When cuttings are made from a plant, it is only at the node that new roots and leaves can grow.

WHERE TO FIND THEM

Find leaves anywhere plants are growing. Grass, shrubs, trees, weeds, and indoor potted plants will all provide leaves for this project.

HOW TO KEEP THEM

You may want to press some brightly colored leaves or even green ones. Before putting them in a heavy book, keep the book from staining by placing the leaves between paper towels. Then put the book under a heavy weight.

ACTIVITIES

1. Grow leaves in water or from cuttings. To grow a plant from a cutting take a portion of the stem with two or more nodes. Cut cleanly below the lowest node and remove any leaves from the stem, both at this place and then at the node above, if there are more than two nodes. Cut any remaining leaves across so that not too great a surface remains for moisture loss to dry out the plant. Now place the stem in sand, loose soil, or specially prepared potting soil. Water thoroughly but after that give only enough water to keep the soil slightly moist. Several such stems may be placed in the same flowerpot. When green leaves have sprouted these cuttings can be removed, each to a small pot, later to be transferred to larger ones.

2. Take a "feel walk", having the children feel the different textures of leaves and bring back some for further handling and observation. Caution: Be sure you avoid poisonous and toxic leaves (see A Feel Walk, pages 1–3).

3. Have the children run a finger around the edges of leaves and note their variety—smooth, saw-edged, lobed, scalloped, prickly, spiny, etc. They can then draw them or do as suggested in item 4.

4. Make leafprints by pressing the leaf, veined side down, on an ink pad. In so doing place a scrap of newspaper over the leaf

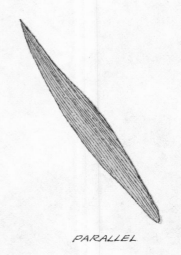

PARALLEL

while running the fingers over it. Then remove the inked leaf to a piece of clean paper, once more covering it with another sheet of paper and rubbing thoroughly with the fingertips.

5. Another method for making a leaf print is to place the leaf underneath a piece of white paper and scribble lightly over the paper with a soft pencil or crayon. This leaf should be placed vein side up. After removing the leaf the paper can be cut to a clean edge.

6. Observe the arrangement of the leaves on the stem of any plant. Are they opposite (two or more at a node) or alternate (one at each node growing on the opposite sides of the stalk). Hold the stalk or twig in the sunlight and observe how each arrange-ment assures the leaves below their quota of sunlight.

7. Roll the stem of the leaf between two fingers to determine its shape—round, flattened, or angled.

8. Observe how the upper and lower surfaces of the leaf differ in color and texture.

9. Feel the surface of the leaf. Is it sticky, furry, sleek, shiny, rough, prominently veined?

10. Look for the three types of veining—parallel as in grass and iris leaves; pinnate, or feather-veined, with a prominent midrib, as in oak or rose leaves; or palmate, with the veins rising at the base of the leaf, as the bones of our fingers meet at the wrist (hence *palm*—ate), as in ivy and geranium leaves.

SOME HELPFUL MATERIALS

crayons
cuttings from plants
indoor potted plants
ink stamp pad
leaves from outdoors
paper towels
sand or potting mix
scissors

KEY VOCABULARY FOR CHILDREN

furry
leaf bud
nodes
rough
shiny
sleek
spiny
stalk
*succulents
veins

*Suggested for older children only

PINNATE

PALMATE

Select for this project a large or single flower, such as a tulip, daffodil, snapdragon, wild rose, pansy, or cyclamen in which the parts can be observed easily. DO NOT SELECT DAISIES, MARGUERITES, ASTERS, ANY OTHER MEMBERS OF THE SUNFLOWER FAMILY, OR CALLA LILIES. The florets on these are so small that it is difficult to handle them and to identify the flower parts (see Dandelions, page 146).

A perfect flower is composed of four so-called floral envelopes, placed one within the encirclement of the others. The outermost envelope, called the calyx (meaning "cup"), is composed of sepals, which serve to protect the unripe bud before it is ready to open. The sepals are often green, though not always. The second floral envelope, known as the corolla, or little crown, is made up of petals. In some flowers these are joined into a tube, as in snapdragons and daffodils, and in others they are separate as in roses and pansies. Their bright colors serve to attract insects or birds to enable them to find the nectar or pollen they are seeking. The odors, too, attract insects and plants that are fertilized by night-flying moths give out a stronger aroma at night.

Within the circle of the petals are the male organs, the stamens, composed of two parts, the anther and the filament. The anther is a pollen producer and the filament is the stalk that supports it.

In the most protected part of a flower is the female organ, the pistil, made up of three parts: the stigma, style, and ovary. The stigma is sticky and pollen adheres to it. The style is a tube down which the sprouting pollen grows, and the ovary is the container of the ovules, or unfertilized seeds. When the pollen reaches the ovules, fertilization takes place, the ovule expands and develops into a seed.

Each species of flower differs from most others in the arrangement and form of these organs, and in their methods of pollination.

WHERE TO FIND THEM

Look for flowers in gardens or in florist shops, where the florist may give you fading flowers, which are as useful for this study as fresh ones. Look also in the fields and on hillsides where wild flowers grow, in vacant lots where weeds, too, put forth flowers and in flowerpots grown indoors.

HOW TO KEEP THEM

It is best to make your observation as soon as you get the flowers. Do not try to examine more than one or two varieties at a time. Flowers can, of course, be kept in water until needed.

ACTIVITIES

1. A magnifying glass will assist in observing the pistil, the ovary, and the stamens. The flowers should be carefully dissected, not torn apart so that the organs are injured.

2. Make some observations on flowers still growing: follow the unfolding of the bud and what happens after the flower has been fertilized and the petals have fallen away, and later how the seeds look and are

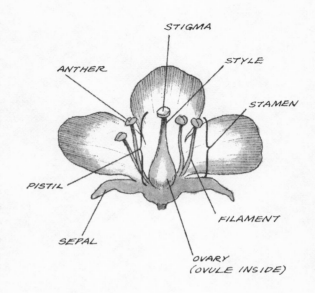

STIGMA

STYLE

ANTHER

STAMEN

PISTIL

FILAMENT

SEPAL

OVARY
(OVULE INSIDE)

distributed. Do this with several different flowers and compare the differences. After a number of the large flowers have been studied, some of the minute ones can also be observed.

3. After examining the flower parts, the children may draw and paint pictures of the flowers. Keep several flowers of the same species—some still intact and some dissected—so that the children can observe both the whole flower and its inner parts as they are making their pictures.

4. Grow some plants, such as geraniums, narcissus, and other spring bulbs. On these, flowers ripen before too long.

5. Save some seeds from the fading flowers, either those grown outside or those grown in the classroom, and plant them. While they probably will not produce flowers within the school year, the children may at least come to realize that seeds produce plants upon which flowers grow.

6. Press some of the flowers in a heavy book under a weight. First put the flowers between paper towels or blotting paper to protect the pages of the book from stain. Change the toweling if the flowers are juicy, replacing it until the flowers are completely dry.

7. Flower dances might be composed with the forms of the flowers incorporated into the costume.

8. The developing flower can be produced in dramatic form.

THIS PROJECT IS PRIMARILY FOR OLDER CHILDREN. IT IS TOO INTENSIVE FOR THE LITTLE ONES.

SOME HELPFUL MATERIALS

books, heavy or magazines
crayons
flowers, large (not sunflower
  or calla lily)
knife
magnifying glasses
paints
paper
pencils
scissors
tumblers
water

KEY VOCABULARY FOR CHILDREN

anther
color
odor
ovary
petals
pollen
seeds
sepals
stigma

Seeds

A seed is a fertilized ovule. Fertilization occurs when pollen reaches the ovary and unites with the ovule inside. Pollen produced by the stamens fertilizes only the same flower or another of the same variety. Pollen is carried to some plants by a live agent, usually an insect, and brought to other plants by the wind. A showy flower usually indicates that it is pollinated by an insect or bird, which visits the flower to obtain the sweet nectar or pollen or both. As the animal dives deep into the nectar, inadvertently some pollen brushes off and adheres to the sticky stigma of the next flower visited. This pollen then grows down into the ovary where fertilization occurs and the ovule develops into a seed.

Seeds are of many shapes and sizes. We eat a number of them such as peas and beans, nuts, poppy seeds, sesame and caraway seeds, as well as the grains which are ground up into flour. The fruits we eat have a pulpy covering around the seeds. The seeds inside are sometimes spread by animals after the fruit is eaten.

Inside the seed are a number of organs: the plumule, or potential shoot; fleshy leaves, called cotyledons, which nourish the sprouting plant until the true leaves can take over. There is also a rudimentary root, the radicle, and surrounding all this are outer coats which protect the seed from premature sprouting in an unfavorable place or under unpropitious conditions.

A seed requires water to break these outer coverings. Once the outer covering is broken the roots grow downwards, anchor the seedling in the ground, and start providing the plant with water and minerals

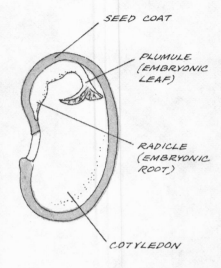

SEED COAT

PLUMULE
(EMBRYONIC
LEAF)

RADICLE
(EMBRYONIC
ROOT)

COTYLEDON

drawn up from below. That is why a seed cannot grow indefinitely in water, even though it is the leaves that serve as the organs for producing nourishment.

WHERE TO FIND THEM

Seeds are available on the kitchen shelf, at the seed or vegetable store, in meadows, woods, and gardens where flowers have gone to seed. Orange, lemon, and other

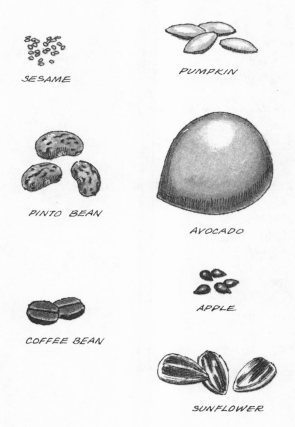

SESAME

PUMPKIN

PINTO BEAN

AVOCADO

COFFEE BEAN

APPLE

SUNFLOWER

citrus fruit seeds will also sprout. Apple, apricot, peach, pear, and cherry pits, melon and squash seeds, nuts (if not too old and dry), and large avocado seeds are all suitable for planting.

(Yams and sweet potatoes, beets, carrots, and turnips are roots, not seeds. Onions and bulbs of other sorts are stems. Potatoes, too, are stems, the "eyes" being the nodes of the stem from which roots and leaves sprout.)

ACTIVITIES

1. Sprout some seeds in water or between dampened surfaces of blotting paper or on cotton, or inside a jar between the glass and a layer of cotton—also wet. In this way the seed can be observed opening to disclose the tiny plant, the root, and the cotyledons (seed leaves), of the sprouting plant. Watch from day to day how the cotyledons shrivel away as the true leaves grow and take over the job of nourishing the seedling.

2. If an outdoor area is available, by all means start a vegetable garden. Radishes and carrots are easy to grow from seeds, sprout quickly, and the radishes are soon ready to be eaten (but seldom soon enough for the youngsters). Therefore it is advisable to have the children pull up a few plants daily and compare each of these with those pulled a few days before in order to observe how the radishes grow in size. Radishes have to be thinned out at any rate to allow room for them to develop symmetrically.

3. Observe the first seed leaves as they come up, then the sprouting of the true leaves. They differ altogether in looks and shape.

4. Compare the true leaves of the carrots and those of the radishes.

5. Make a collection of seeds and plant some of each in the room. Do not place them too near the radiator and cover them until they sprout. Water the soil well before planting but do not overwater after that. The soil should be kept damp but never wet.

6. Look on the ground under an oak tree for acorns. You may find some that are already sprouting. Try to sprout some yourself, though they are slow in germinating.

7. Shake a pine cone for the seeds to spill out. Look for the wing on pine seeds. It serves to carry them away from the shade of the parent tree.

8. Look under a maple tree for the butterfly-shaped double seeds, called samaras, or for the button balls containing seeds of the sycamores.

9. Plant some citrus fruit and apple seeds, and squash, watermelon, and bean seeds. For planting use small containers such as frozen juice cans (poke a hole in the bottom for drainage), small flowerpots, or Styrofoam cups. Put each variety of seed in a different container.

10. Visit a lawn, field, or meadow and look for seeds that can fly, such as those of dandelions, thistles, and milkweed and let the children blow them about observing the white pappus that carries them aloft.

11. Look for seeds that "hook a ride", such as wild oats, filaree, clover, and various burrs.

12. Let the children make drawings of their plants from time to time to observe the changes in size and shape.

SOME HELPFUL MATERIALS

blotting paper
cans, frozen juice
cotton
cups, Styrofoam
jars
seeds of many varieties
soil
water

KEY VOCABULARY FOR CHILDREN

acorns
*cotyledon
flower
pollen
root
seed coat
sprout

*Suggested for older children only

The dandelion belongs to a group of flowers called composites, so named because each bloom is actually a group of flowers, or florets, crowded together in a "head." Daisylike flowers of every sort belong to this composite group. (See Flowers, page 139.)

The typical composite is formed of two sorts of florets, ray and disc. The ray flowers are those one pulls off when asking the flower whether "he loves me or loves me not." The disc florets are those in the center of the head and are often yellow in color.

The dandelion has only ray flowers, which are strap-shaped, each containing all the organs of a perfect flower: stamens, pistil, and ovary. Surrounding all the florets are numerous green bracts that act as a protection for the unripe flowers.

Dandelion stems are hollow and bare of leaves and contain a milky juice.

The leaves that grow at the base of the stem in a rosette have jagged and variously lobed edges. When a dandelion goes to seed it produces a little parachute from which the seed is suspended, while being carried away by the wind. The parachute is composed of a white or brown pappus, similar to thistledown, and is spun around by the wind so that when it finally lands on the ground the seed is screwed firmly into the soil. When all the seeds have blown away, a flat, white receptacle remains on the stem.

INDIVIDUAL FLOWER (FLORET)

PARACHUTE

WHERE TO FIND THEM

Find dandelions on the lawn and in fields, in low, damp places. These are very common flowers, usually rated as weeds.

ACTIVITIES

1. Examine growing dandelions, noticing the pointed bud of the unopened flower. Tear it apart to see how the florets are folded inside.

2. Observe and compare the shapes of different leaves. Feel around the edges and then cut them from the plant and superimpose one upon another to recognize the diversity of shapes.

3. In the early spring the leaves are tender and are eaten for salad. Let the children taste them.

4. After the pappus has appeared let the children blow the seeds away, noting how and where they fall to the ground.

5. Examine the little seed suspended below the pappus and note its pointed lower end.

6. Plant some dandelion seeds in a pot and some in water or between the sides of a glass tumbler and a wad of cotton, or upon damp blotters or cotton. Watch them all sprout and see how long the seeds growing in water will continue to live. (See Seeds, pages 141–144.)

7. Pick a dandelion to pieces and examine the strap-shaped florets through a magnifying glass to identify the stamens and pistil.

8. Break the stalk of a growing dandelion and observe the milky juice.

9. Look for dandelions in various places—flower beds, grass, etc., and discuss why they are found here.

10. Peel off the outer skin of the stem. It will form curls. Note that the stem is in several layers.

11. Try to uproot a dandelion plant in order to find out how firmly it is anchored in the ground. This is one reason for its success as a plant.

12. Dig up the root with a spade and examine the long, woody root, and the root hairs through which the water enters. It is the root that holds the plant fast in the ground.

13. Make whistles from the hollow stems by holding them in front of the mouth and blowing across the top.

14. Let the children compose a dandelion seed dance, moving here and there on tiptoes with outstretched arms, like the pappus, and the feet close together, like the suspended seed.

SOME HELPFUL MATERIALS

blotters
cotton
flowerpots or Styrofoam cups
tumbler, clear glass or plastic

KEY VOCABULARY FOR CHILDREN

*pappus
*pistil
 pollen
 root
 ray
 seed ball
 seeds
 stalk
*stamen
*thistledown

*Suggested for older children only

A Lawn

Most lawns contain a number of different plants. There are sometimes several varieties of grass, clover, chickweed, dandelion, common plantain, pineapple weed, daisies, and many others. In order to differentiate between these plants one must get down and observe them closely. All of them bear flowers, some of which may not be recognized as such. Grass flowers are inconspicuous and are wind pollinated, having no need for showy flowers to attract insects to effect fertilization. (See Flowers, pages 138–140.)

Grass leaves are long and slender and clasp the stem. Their veining is parallel, running straight from the base to the tip.

Chickweed, clover, dandelions, daisies, and pineapple weed all bear conspicuous flowers. Of these dandelions (see Dandelions, pages 145–147), pineapple weed, and daisies all belong to the composite group of flowers. The composites have a number of florets crowded into a tight cluster.

Common plantain, not a composite, grows like the dandelion out of a rosette of leaves on a long stalk. The veins of these leaves meet at the base of the leaf and are therefore not parallel. The flowers are very small and white in color.

Chickweed has a tiny starlike flower and its stems are weak and slender and covered with minute hairs.

The clovers can be identified by their compound leaves composed of three or four leaflets. There are a number of clovers that invade our lawns, each differing from the others, either in size or color or markings of the leaves.

WHERE TO FIND IT

Any lawn will do—the one around the school house, or in a park, or at someone's house.

ACTIVITIES

1. Sit down on the lawn and pick out as many different varieties of plants as you can find. These can be identified primarily by the leaves but also by the flowers.
2. Look for the veining of the leaves: parallel; pinnate, with a midrib and the veins branching off, like a feather in form; palmate—all large veins meeting at the base of the leaf as the bones of one's fingers do at the wrist (hence *palm*-ate).
3. Make leaf prints of the three types (see Leaves, pages 136–137).

PLANTAIN

CHICKWEED

CLOVER

149

4. Look for the flowers on the grasses, and if you can find different varieties, compare them. (These are best found on a lawn that has not been recently mowed.)

5. Look for different species of clover. Each has characteristic coloring and leaves.

6. Bur clover has leaflets with small whitish spots and dark red spots. Its flowers are yellow. The seed pod is coiled into a flat doughnut. Unwind the prickled edge and you will find the seeds inside.

7. Try to uproot a dandelion by tugging on the leaves. You will find that this is almost impossible to do unless the soil is very wet, but you can dig it up. Then note the long, strong root that anchors it to the ground.

8. Daisies on a lawn can be picked and made into daisy chains with a thread wound around the stems.

9. Chickweed is eaten by birds, so if you have a canary, place some in its cage. Look for the tiny wrinkled seeds.

10. Be on the lookout for any animals crawling among the grasses. There may be beetles, earthworms, grasshoppers, and many others.

11. Plant some birdseed or grass seed in a flowerpot. Birdseed will produce grasses and should yield interesting comparisons with the grasses growing in the lawn.

SOME HELPFUL MATERIALS

birdseed
flowerpots or Styrofoam cups
grass seed
magnifying glasses
soil
thread
trowels or flat knives

KEY VOCABULARY FOR CHILDREN

chickweed
clover
*composite flowers
daisies
dandelions
head
leaflets
pineapple weed
plantain
veining

*Suggested for older children only

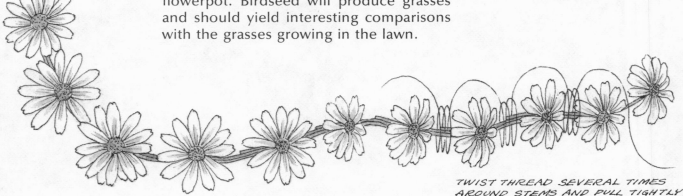

TWIST THREAD SEVERAL TIMES
AROUND STEMS AND PULL TIGHTLY

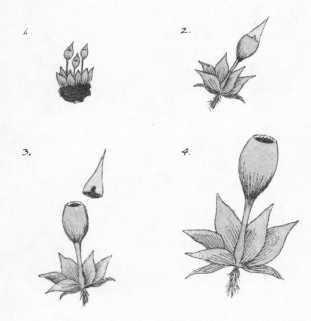

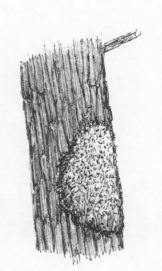

Moss is a nonflowering plant which grows in many places, even between the curbstone and the pavement of a city street. Its tiny, green leaves indicate that it is self-supporting. It produces its own nourishment from carbon dioxide in the air combined with water, which is absorbed by the thin rootlike structures that fasten it to the ground.

The reproductive cycle of mosses is a complicated one. To start, the spores are tiny dustlike particles that differ from seeds in that they carry no nourishment for the sprouting plant. The spore is produced in a spore case which is carried on a thin stalk, elevated above the moss plant. This spore case sheds its spores when the cap that covers it falls off to reveal a row of tiny teeth around the inside edge of the spore case. When wet these teeth contract and bend down into the spores, which stick to them.

As the teeth become dry they shrink and turn outward, where they can release their spores to the wind. When the spores now fall upon favorable, damp ground, the resulting growth is green and threadlike. From this grows the leafy plant which we know as moss, which in turn bears the spores in the tiny uplifted spore case.

Mosses will shrivel up in a hot, dry spell, but as soon as they receive moisture will once more turn green and continue to grow.

WHERE TO FIND THEM

Mosses grow on wood or stone in shady places and can also be found on stone and brick walls, on the ground, under trees, or on the bark of trees, and even in flowerpots, if the soil has been kept moist.

HOW TO KEEP THEM

Mosses can be easily grown in dish gardens or in closed jars, their sole requirement being a cool spot and a thin layer of rich soil upon which to grow. They must, however, be kept moist, but too much water will encourage the growth of mildew which will kill the moss.

ACTIVITIES

1. Make a collection of as many varieties of mosses as you can find. Start each in a separate container.

2. Compare the tiny leaves, the spore cases, and the general shape the growing plant assumes—moundlike, flat, spreading, etc.

3. Use a magnifying glass to look for the spore cases on mosses growing outdoors. They are usually brown, not much larger than the top of a pin, and held aloft by a thin filament often brown in color. Examine the moss leaves and spore cases and see if you can find the tiny teeth that ring the inside edge of the case and the little cap which covers the case.

4. Pick off the spore cases with tweezers and pry the lids off with a pin. Then shake out the spores and sow them on the surface of some damp soil.

5. Mosses are suitable for terrariums but can be planted as little gardens, either in a shallow bowl or dish or a covered container. In the latter a glass or transparent cover is desirable and the garden will seldom require watering, but the lid must be raised when the glass "sweats" on the inside to prevent mildew from forming. Furnish either type of container with a layer of soil, a rock or two, or a bit of bark and keep it damp.

6. You can dry pieces of moss for preserving by pressing them between paper toweling under the weight of a heavy object. See that the pressure is evenly distributed. When dry the specimen can be mounted on paper with gummed tape.

SOME HELPFUL MATERIALS

book, heavy
cap
jars or aquaria or other
   containers
magnifying glasses
pins
rocks
soil, garden
tape, gummed
tweezers
water

KEY VOCABULARY FOR CHILDREN

*rootlike structures
 spore case
 spores
 tiny teeth

*Suggested for older children only

Bibliography

FOR ADULTS

Beck, Barbara *The First Book of Weeds*, New York, Franklin Watts Inc., 1963.

Brockman, C. Frank *Trees of North America*, New York, Western Publishing Co., Inc., 1968.

Dowden, Anne *Look at a Flower*, New York, Thomas Y. Crowell Co., 1963.

Hammond, Winifred *The Riddle of Seeds*, New York, Coward, McCann and Geoghegan, Inc., 1966.

Hutchins, Ross E. *Plants Without Leaves*, New York, Dodd, Mead & Co., 1966.

Hutchins, Ross E. *The Amazing Seeds*, New York, Dodd, Mead & Co., 1965.

Hutchins, Ross E. *This Is a Leaf*, New York, Dodd, Mead & Co., 1962.

Hutchins, Ross E. *This Is a Tree*, New York, Dodd, Mead & Co., 1964.

Lane, Ferdinand C. *All About the Flowering World*, New York, Random House, Inc., 1956.

Life (periodical) *The Forest*, New York, Time-Life Books, 1963.

Life (periodical) *The Plants*, New York, Time-Life Books, 1963.

Nickelsburg, Janet *Field Trips; Ecology For Youth Leaders*, Minneapolis, Minn., Burgess Publishing Co., 1966.

Riedman, Sarah R. *World Provider: The Story of Grass*, New York, Abelard-Schuman, Ltd., 1962.

Selsam, Millicent E. *Play with Seeds*, New York, William Morrow & Co., Inc., 1957.

Selsam, Millicent E. *Play with Trees*, New York, William Morrow & Co., Inc. 1950.

Selsam, Millicent E. *Seeds and More Seeds*, New York, Harper & Row, Publishers Inc., 1959.

Shuttleworth, Floyd S. and Herbert S. Zim *Non-Flowering Plants*, New York, Western Publishing Co., Inc., 1967.

Sterling, Dorothy *Story of Mosses, Ferns, and Mushrooms*, Garden City, N.Y., Doubleday & Co., Inc. 1955.

Zim, Herbert S. and Alexander C. Martin *Trees: A Guide to Familiar American Trees*, New York, Western Publishing Co., Inc., 1952.

FOR CHILDREN

Bancroft, Henrietta *Down Come the Leaves,* New York, Thomas Y. Crowell Co., 1961.

Blough, Glenn O. *The Tree on the Road to Turntown,* New York, McGraw-Hill Book Co., 1953.

Bulla, Clyde Robert *A Tree Is a Plant,* New York, Thomas Y. Crowell Co., 1960.

Jordan, Helene J. *How a Seed Grows,* New York, Thomas Y. Crowell Co., 1960.

Jordan, Helene J. *Seeds by Wind and Water,* New York, Thomas Y. Crowell Co., 1962.

Langstaff, John and Feodor Rojankovsky *Over in the Meadow,* New York, Harcourt Brace Jovanovich, Inc., 1967.

Lerner, Sharon *I Found a Leaf,* Minneapolis, Minn., Lerner Publications Co., 1964.

Webber Irma E. *Bits that Grow Big,* Reading, Mass., Addison-Wesley Publishing Co., Inc., 1949.

Webber, Irma E. *Up Above and Down Below,* Reading, Mass., Addison-Wesley Publishing Co., Inc., 1943.

Webber, Irma E. *Travellers All,* Reading, Mass., Addison-Wesley Publishing Co., Inc., 1944.

Zion, Gene *The Plant Sitter,* New York, Harper & Row, Publishers Inc., 1959.

In Conclusion

In concluding this book, I would like to remind you of a few ideas that I have tried to stress. Nature study is primarily another outlet into the world around us—the world that, because of complex conditions of modern life, is gradually being shut off from us. Because the study of nature is no longer available to us simply by opening our back door on a prairie or farm, because for many of us the rising hills no longer meet our eyes, nor the stars descend to our horizons, we must see to it that we hold onto what nature there is left for our children.

The appeal of nature lies somewhere within us all. Why? We say because of its simplicity. But nature isn't simple. It is even more complex than the difficulties we think we are getting away from. Then what is it? To me, the appeal in nature is that one meets it alone, with one's own resources, with one's own appreciations, and that it speaks to you and to me and to each child "in a various language."

What nature says to the four-year-old who asks what makes some leaves yellow and others green, what it says to the feather collector, what it says to the child who watches an egg crack and release a downy chick, neither you nor I can evaluate. Nature talks directly to each of us. That is why, when we help the children to see more, we must be careful not to obscure their own vision with a multitude of facts, so that instead of clarifying we bemuddle, instead of adding to their pleasure we step between them and their own feelings.

Children are entitled to find out what sort of people they are. They will never do so unless you look upon your contacts with them as a fragile privilege. How wonderful to become aware of another's awareness! How fine to be able to expose children to experiences without the intrusion of yourself into them. It is a rare thing to be the confidant of a child; it is rarer still to be a happy sharer of a child's experiences.

Nature study, as I understand it, is but a vehicle. It is not a thing in itself; it is a means of freeing children from predigested thoughts and environments. It is a means by which children are able to come in contact with things that appeal to them without the interference of man's inventions and interventions. It offers the child, and you too, raw material for creating. The out-of-doors offers that greatest of all treasures—the fulfillment of the esthetic urge, which translated into action produces man, the creator.

Janet Nickelsburg

Acknowledgements

PHOTOGRAPHS

P. 4   J. Berger-National Audubon Society Collection/Photo Researchers, Inc.
P. 10   Grant Heilman
P. 15   J. Clawson-National Audubon Society Collection/Photo Researchers, Inc.
P. 18   Gordon S. Smith-National Audubon Society Collection/Photo Researchers, Inc.
P. 22   L. Rue IV-National Audubon Society Collection/Photo Researchers, Inc.
P. 25   Carson Baldwin, Jr.-Animals, Animals © 1975
P. 38   Karl Maslowski-National Audubon Society Collection/Photo Researchers, Inc.
P. 44   Stephen Dalton © 1973-National Audubon Society Collection/Photo Researchers, Inc.
P. 47   Jack Dermid-National Audubon Society Collection/Photo Researchers, Inc.
P. 87   L. Chace-National Audubon Society Collection/Photo Researchers, Inc.
P. 90   L. Rue III-National Audubon Society Collection/Photo Researchers, Inc.
P. 94   Carson Baldwin, Jr.,-Animals, Animals © 1975
P. 97   R. Erwin-National Audubon Society Collection/Photo Researchers, Inc.
P. 120   M. W. F. Tweedle-National Audubon Society Collection/Photo Researchers, Inc.
P. 123   John Gerard-National Audubon Society Collection/Photo Researchers, Inc.
P. 138   R. Curbow-National Audubon Society Collection/Photo Researchers, Inc.

ARTWORK

Margaret Sanfilippo